Written by Kayla E. Willis
Photography by Kayla E. Willis

Published by Wild Lark Books

Wild Lark Books
513 Broadway Street
Lubbock, Texas 79401

Learn More About the Author at wildlarkbooks.com

#supportartreadbooks

POETRY | PHOTOGRAPHY SHOWCASE
ISBN 9781957864808

WILD LARK BOOKS
BOOKSHOP & PUBLISHER

Wild Lark Books is an independent publisher that supports authors as artists.
As with all works of art, reviews help build readerships and increase the impact of this book.

If Kayla's work has inspired you, please help support her artistry by leaving ratings & reviews online, sharing about this book on social media using the hashtag of the title (#psihopethishelps), or speaking about it to your friends and family.

Your support means the world to us.

Thank you!

Wild Lark Books
Support Art. Read Books.

Learn More at WILDLARKBOOKS.COM

p.s. i hope this helps

kayla e. willis

dedicated to the person reading this:
in case you were doubting it today, **you are enough.**

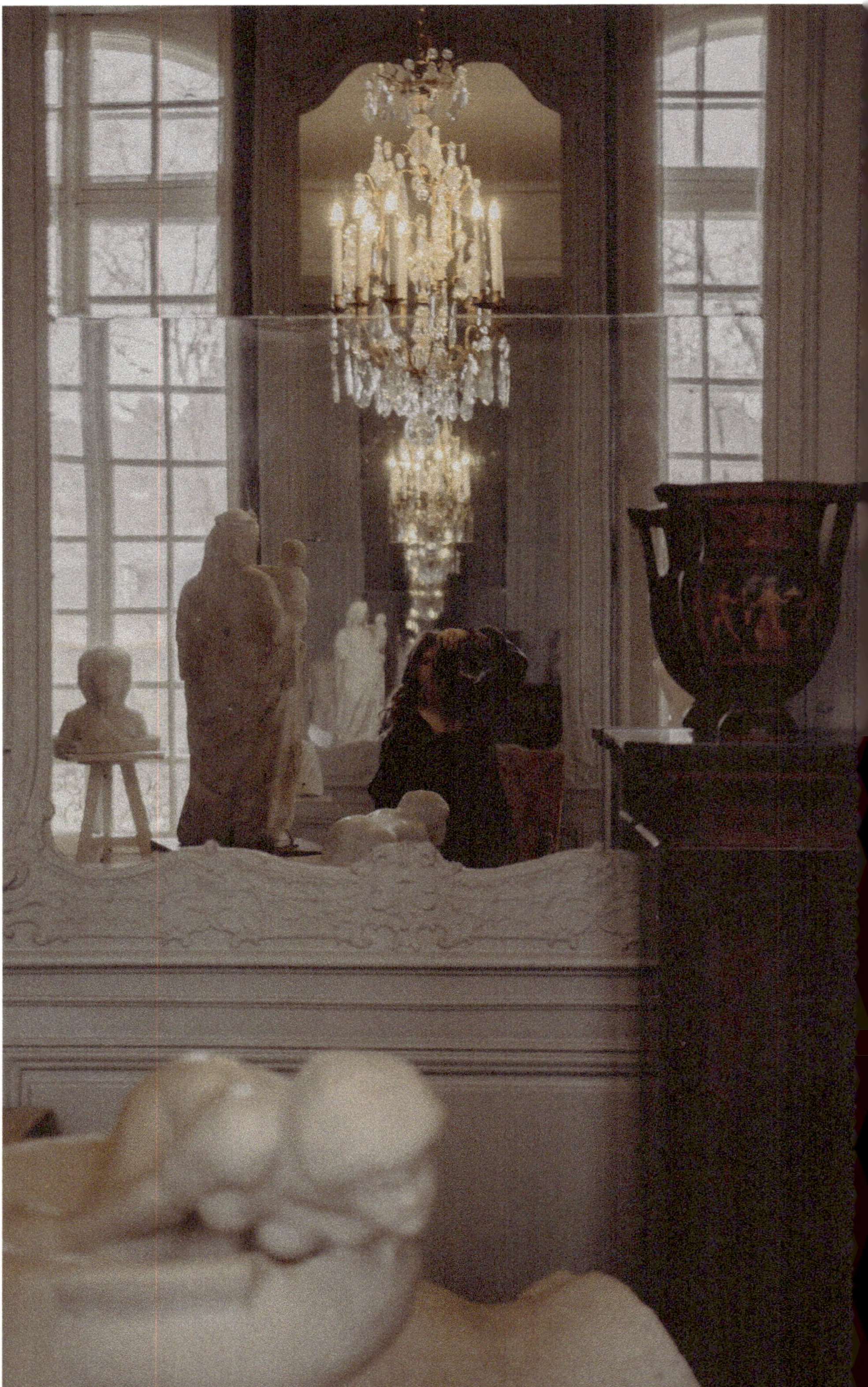

from one soul to another

i often feel incredibly drawn to share the ramblings that come to my soul.
not because i believe i have divine wisdom to express
or because i have something profound to say that will alter and influence the human race.
but because in some moments of my life,
i feel utterly convicted to share the words existing within me.
because i know in the grand scheme of things,
life has no definable meaning.
i am aware that every person is eventually forgotten.
every second we live is a second closer to death.
but isn't that what makes life worth living?
isn't knowing that any moment could be our last
what makes life so sweet?
seconds add up and they turn into minutes that turn into memories.
we won't always be remembered, so why don't we just live
to remember who we were at that exact moment in time,
to make life have a purpose,
to wring every essence of joy out of this life, making it worth living.
i find comfort in my wondering because if i did not know how it felt to live without purpose,
i would not know how it felt to live with purpose.
these are my moments that turned to memories.
the seconds that give my life purpose, captured.
these are the convictions of my soul.

kayla e. willis

and if you want to fall in love, just let me know, because i think i'd be ok with that.

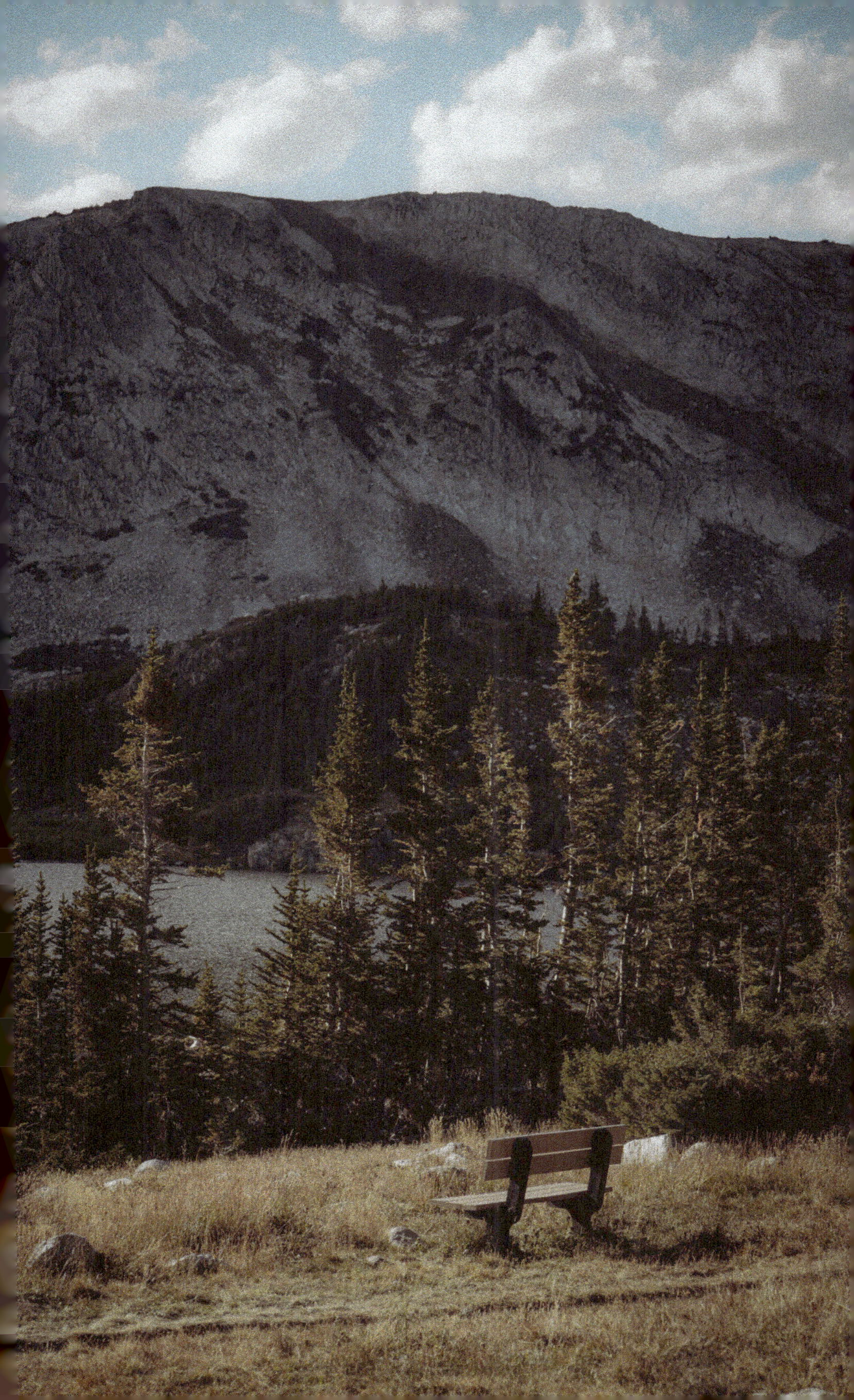

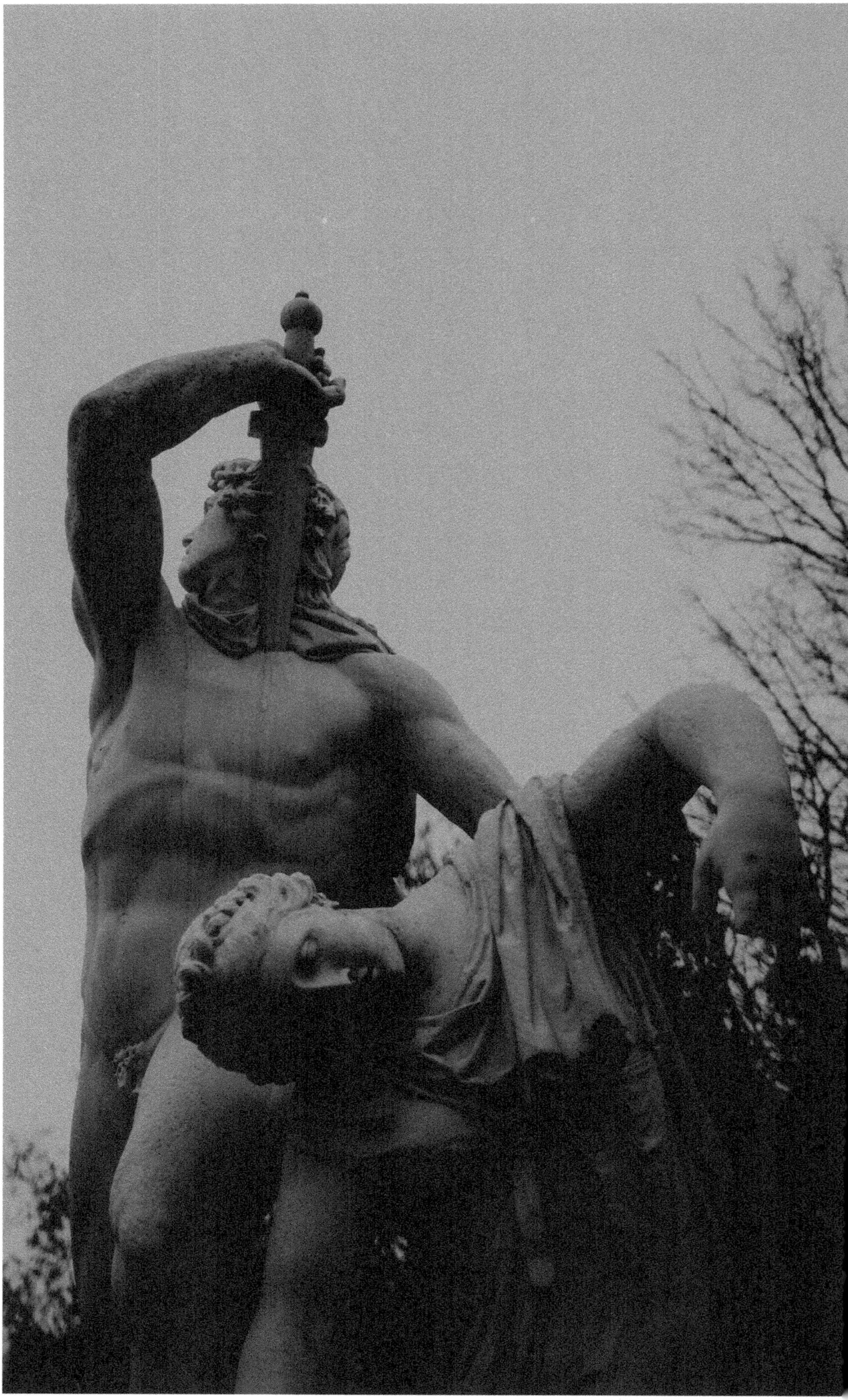

almost

the precipice of almost is the space in which life nests,
we almost touched,
we felt the desire to brush our fingers gently over the skin of another, but chose not to,
we rested in the beautiful pain of words unspoken,
thoughts unsaid,
hearts never embraced or broken

we saw every smile,
laughed at every joke,
became close in a way only hearts yearning for each other can.
we read the signs,
heard the aching between the lines,
talked every moment over with a friend,
and left unanswered in the end.

we felt the sparks,
within our hearts,
but chose not to act.
we chose to protect ourselves.

blame the timing.
choose to ignore the chemistry igniting.
keep up the walls our souls are fighting.

and spend the rest of our life begging the question,
    did you love me as i loved you?
    do you still dream of me too?
    in this disaster of an existence we call life could we have made it through?

but the words stay unsaid,
the words left unread,
the skin left untouched,
the hearts remain crushed,
    the damnable misery of almost.

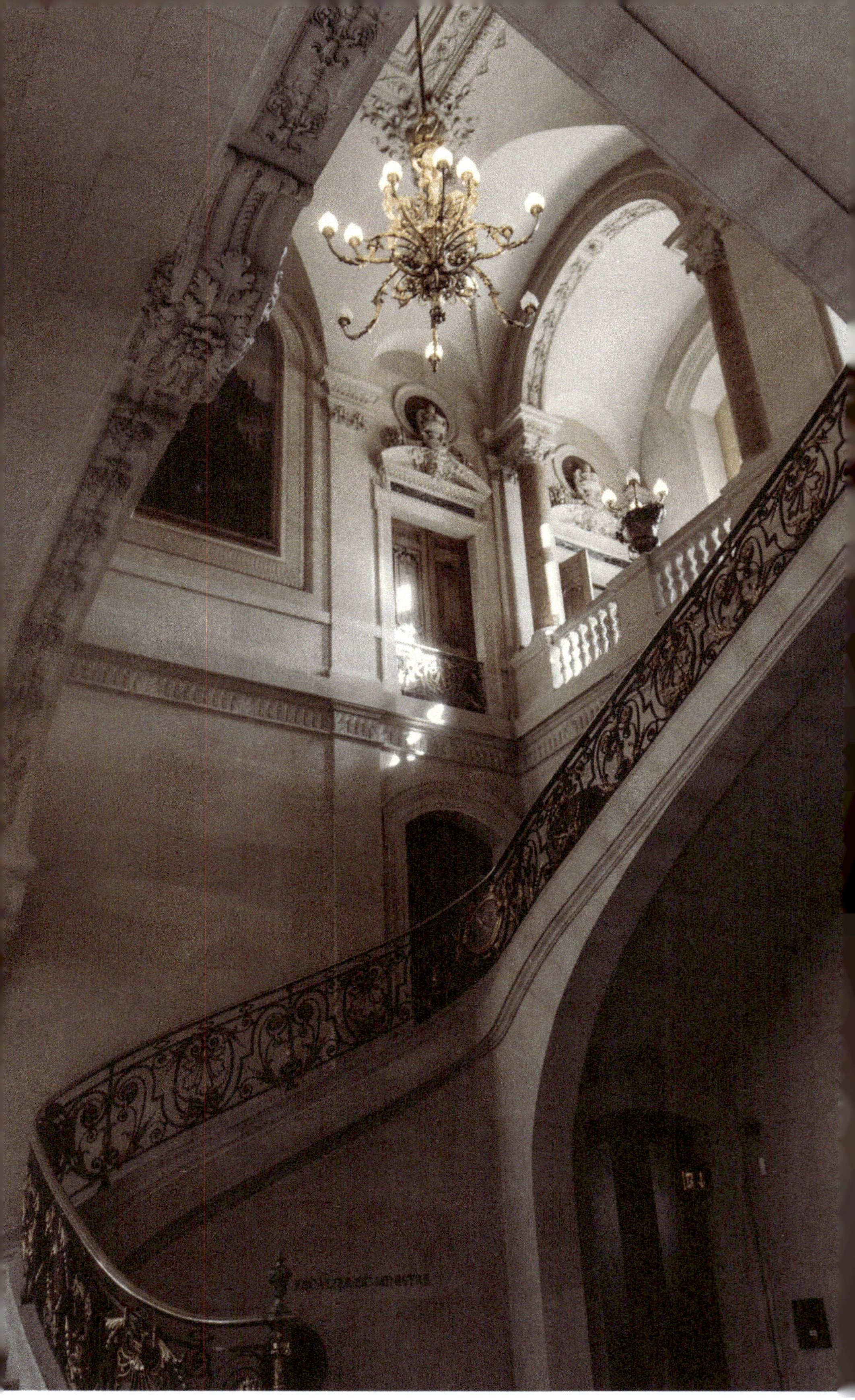

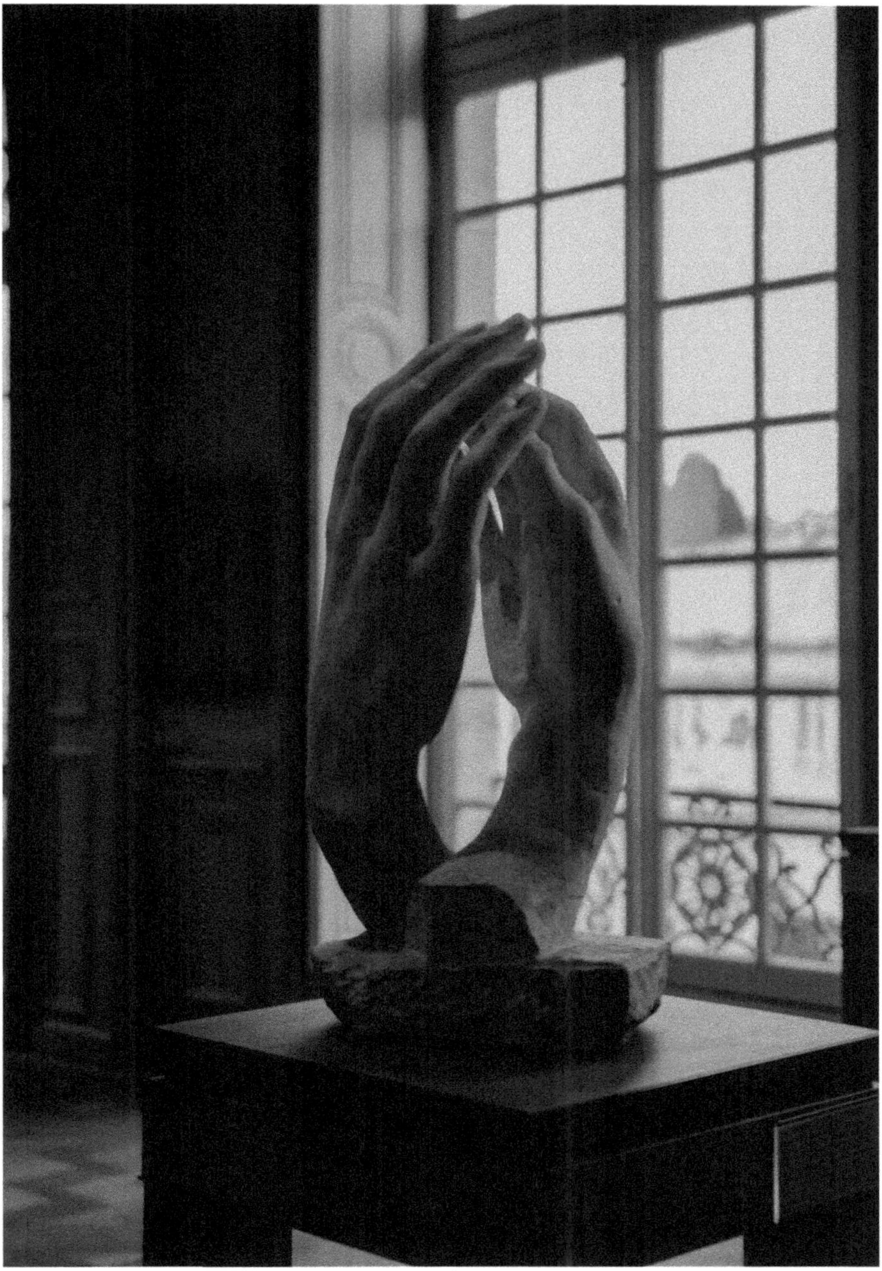

life is far too short for you to not say how you feel.

it's just simply that my heart wants to feel at home again.

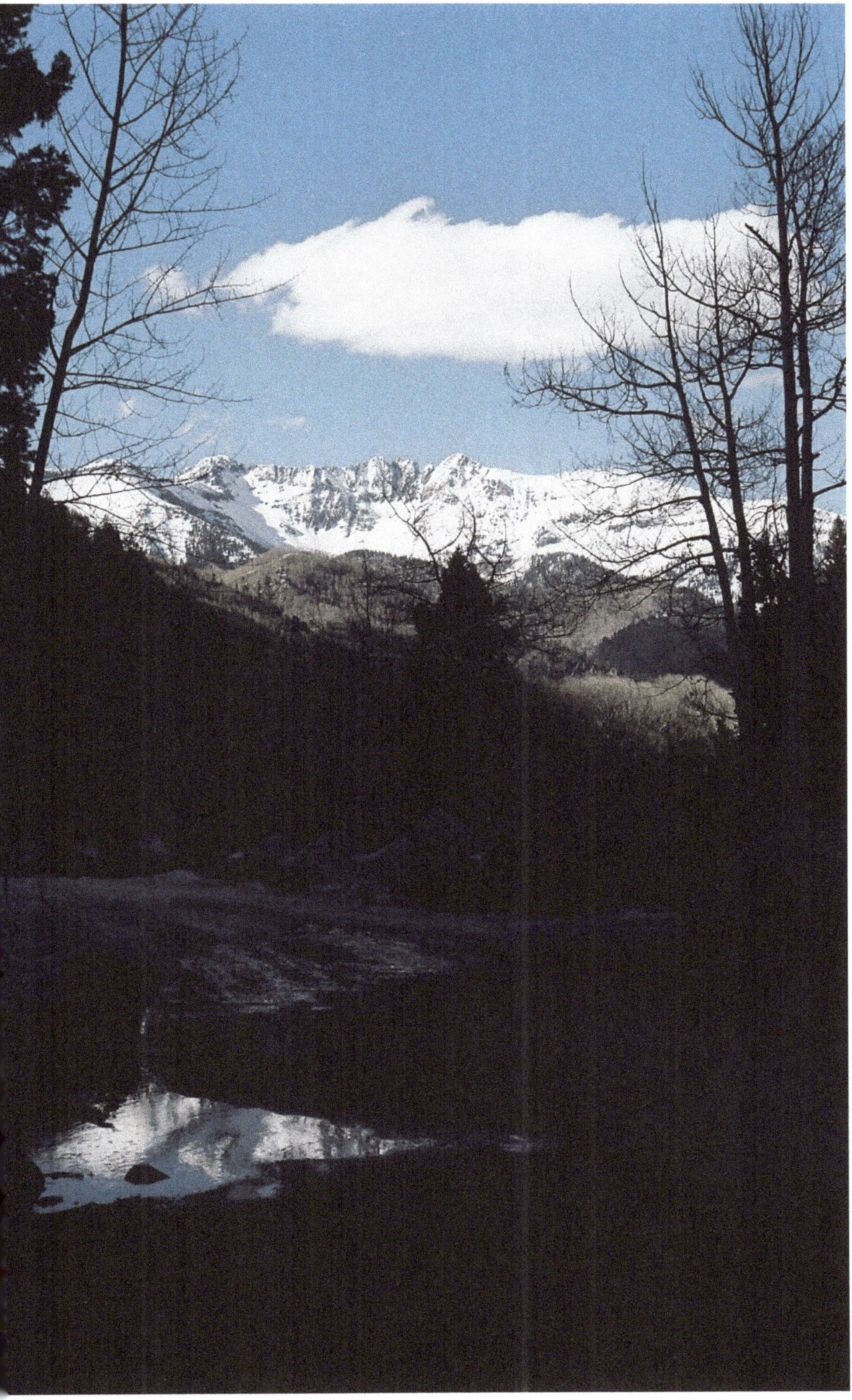

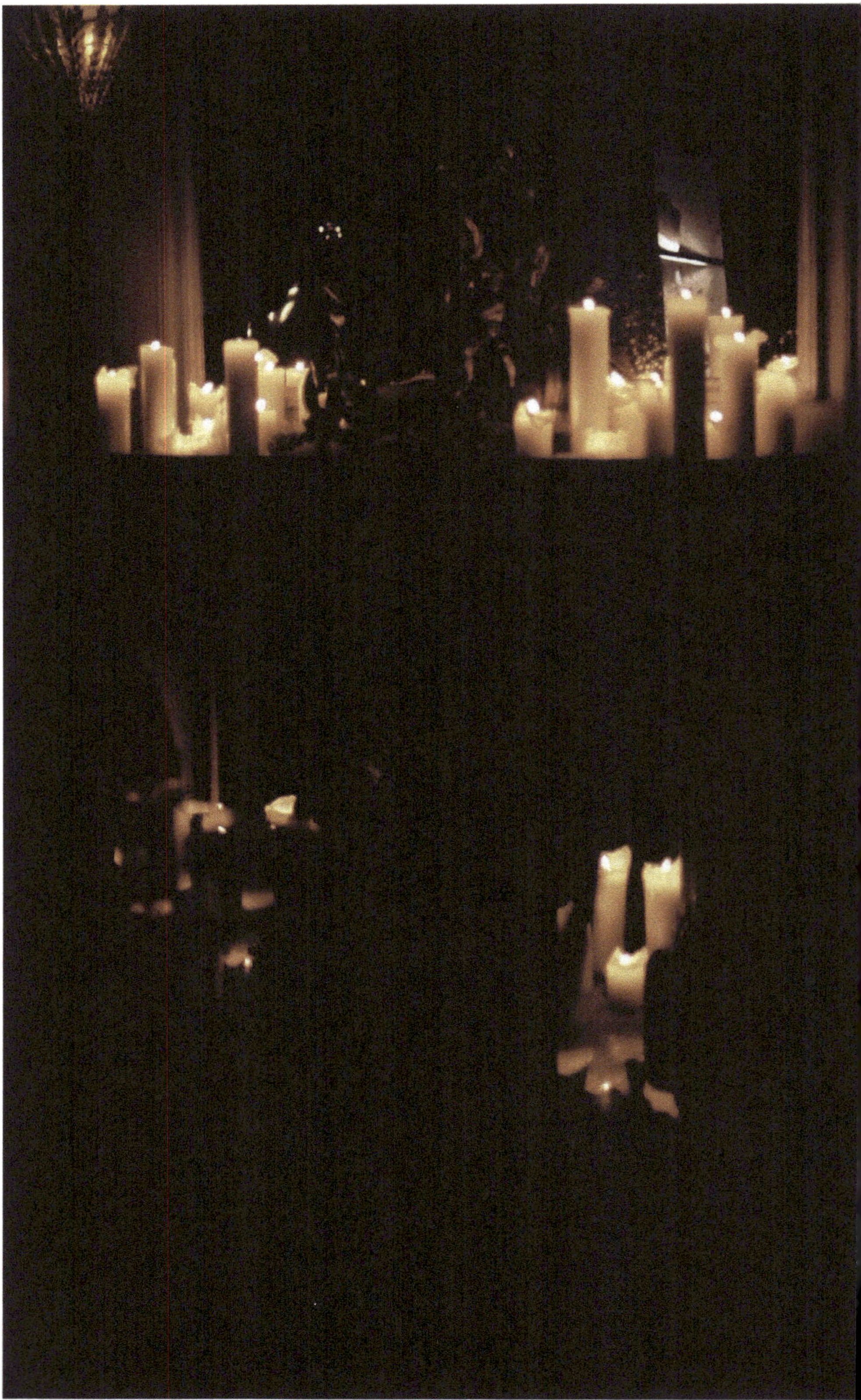

flicker

the flame continues to dance,
despite any circumstance.
so is the fate of a candle.
the wick and wax so in need of one another
unable to survive without the other.
they sacrifice themselves to fuel their heat
and in the process damn their very own existence.
so entranced with each other,
burning themselves to the ground.

the world is on fire
and we are the flames.
i burn for you.
dance with me before we are nothing.

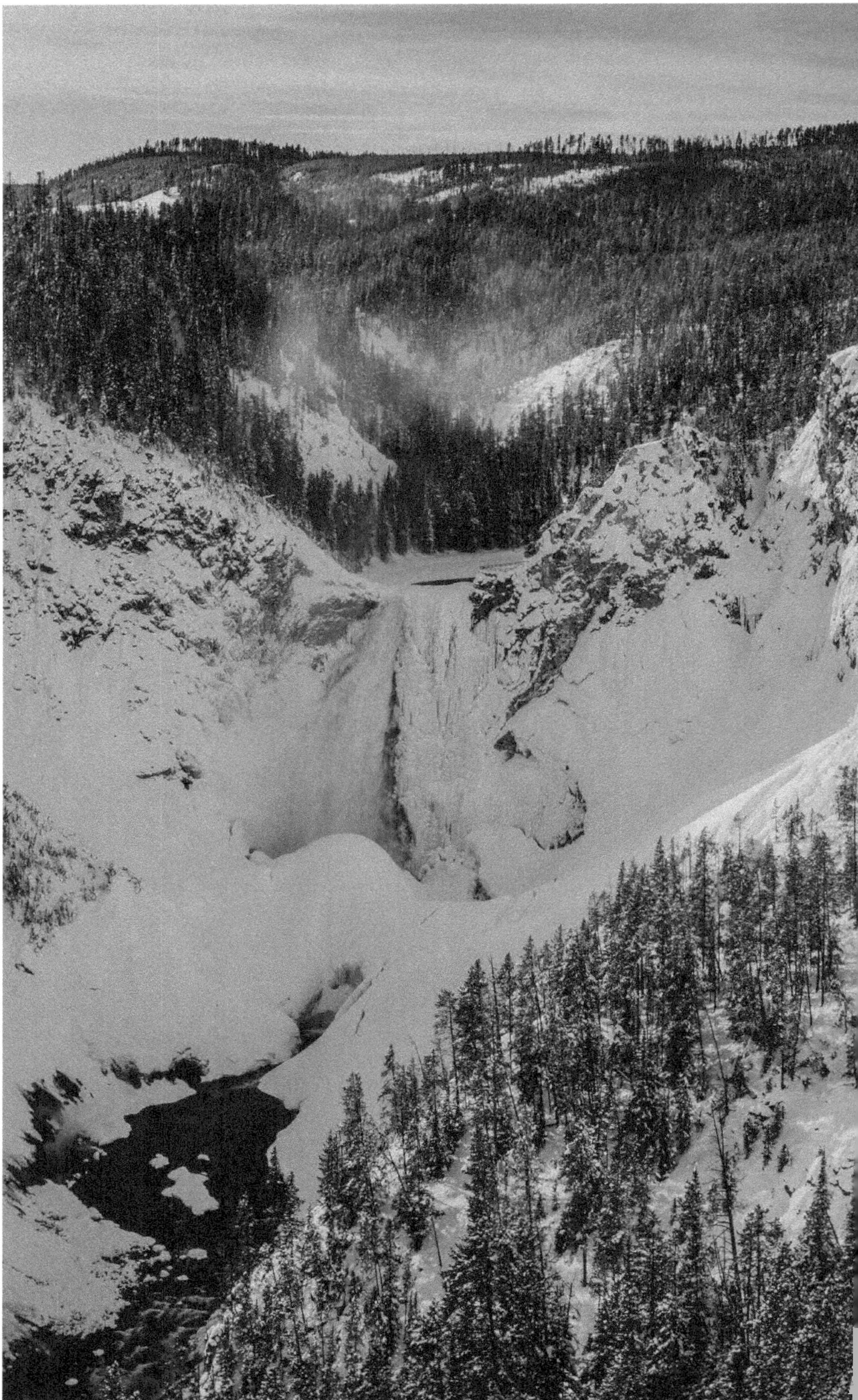

some say love strikes them like lightning, but to me, your love feels like the first sip of coffee on a cold day. a warmth that once on my lips spreads joy throughout my whole body.

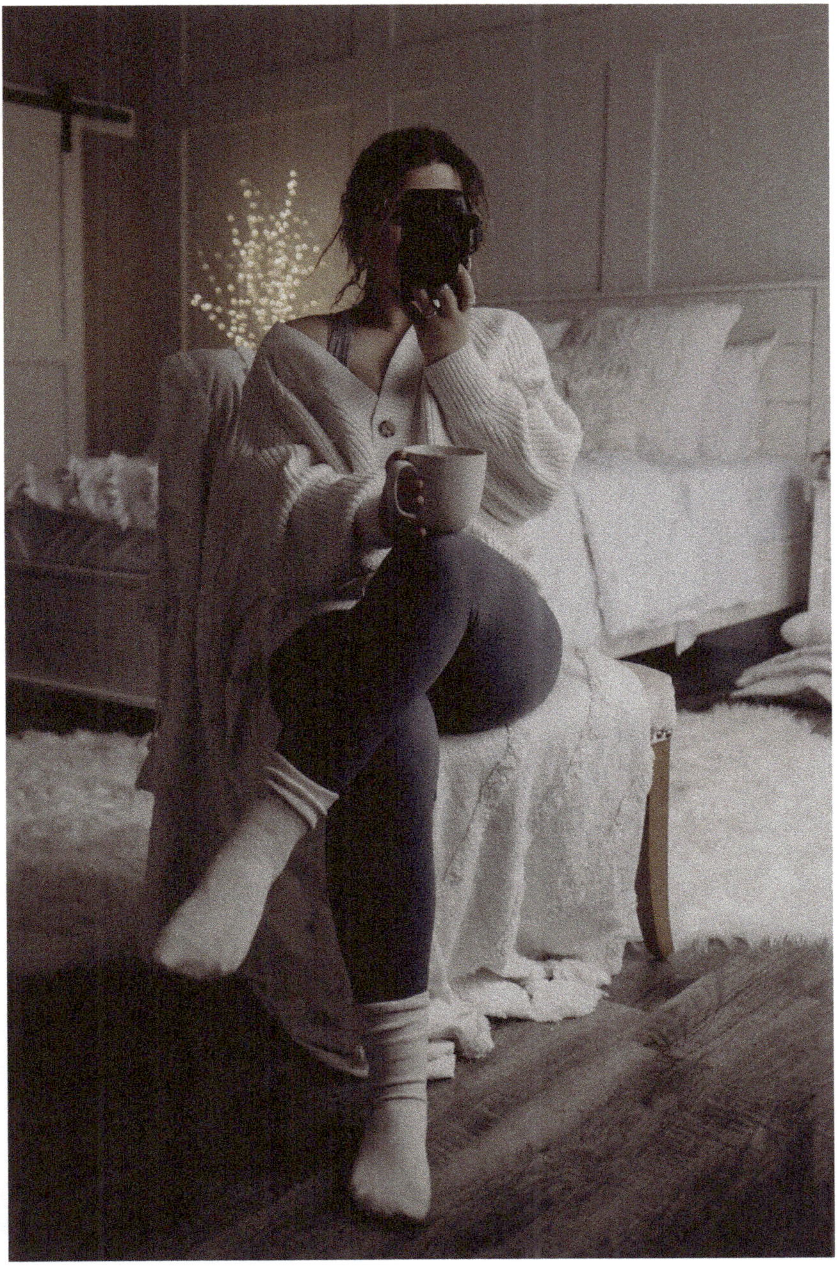

crossed constellations

i told the stars about you.
as they went shooting past,
wishing for what i already have.

i told the stars about you.
resting in your arms with my head on your chest,
in the still perfect silence of the night.
i watched them sparkle and dance in heaven far away,

then turned and saw them in your eyes

and i was reminded of a time long ago,
leaning out of my window,
gazing at the sky.
hoping for a love like you.

and in that moment of telling the stars about you,
the stars leaned down and whispered,
"your wish did come true."

so, i will keep wishing on the stars
because they brought me straight to you.

life is not infinite, and i want to spend every day and every moment with you.

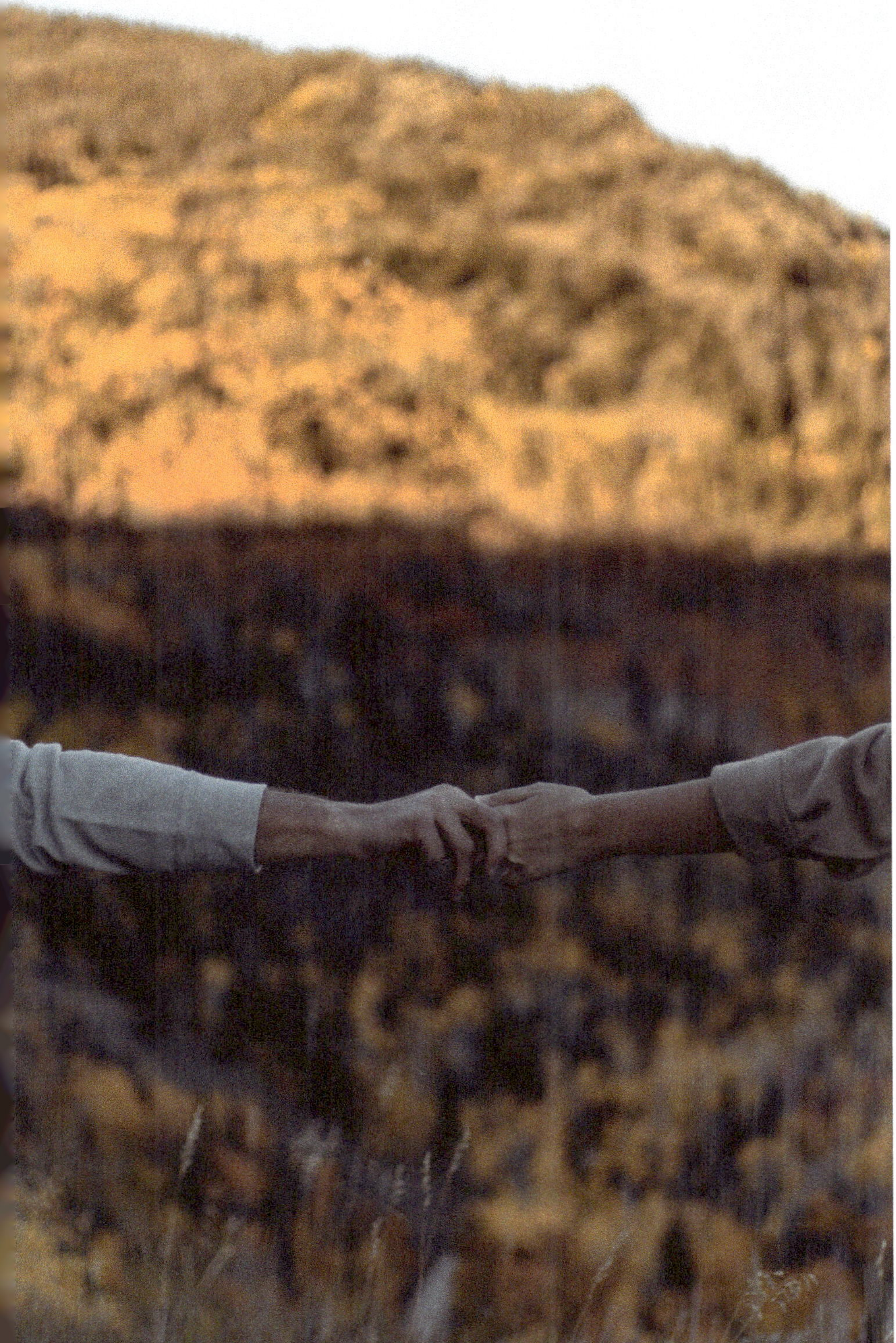

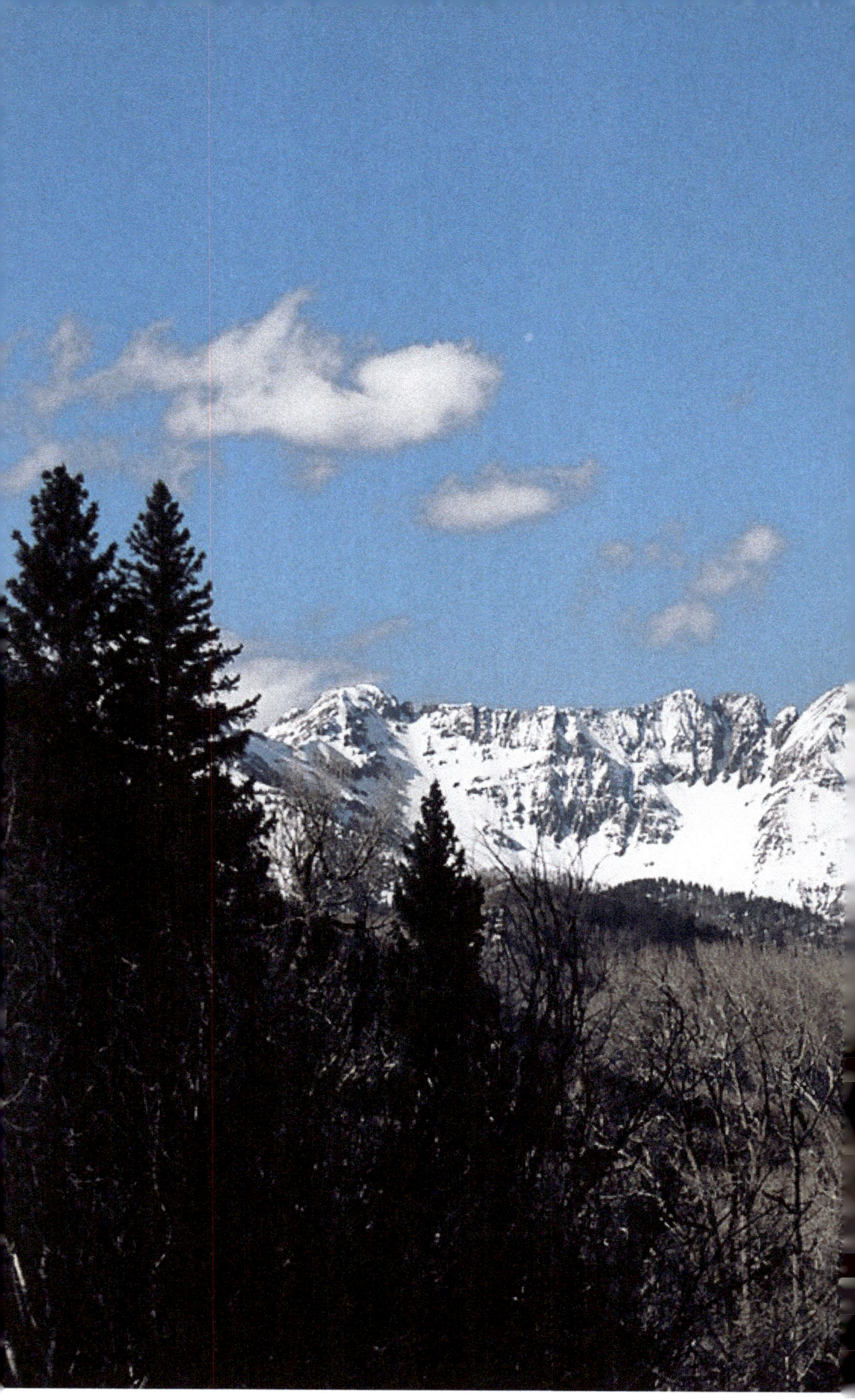

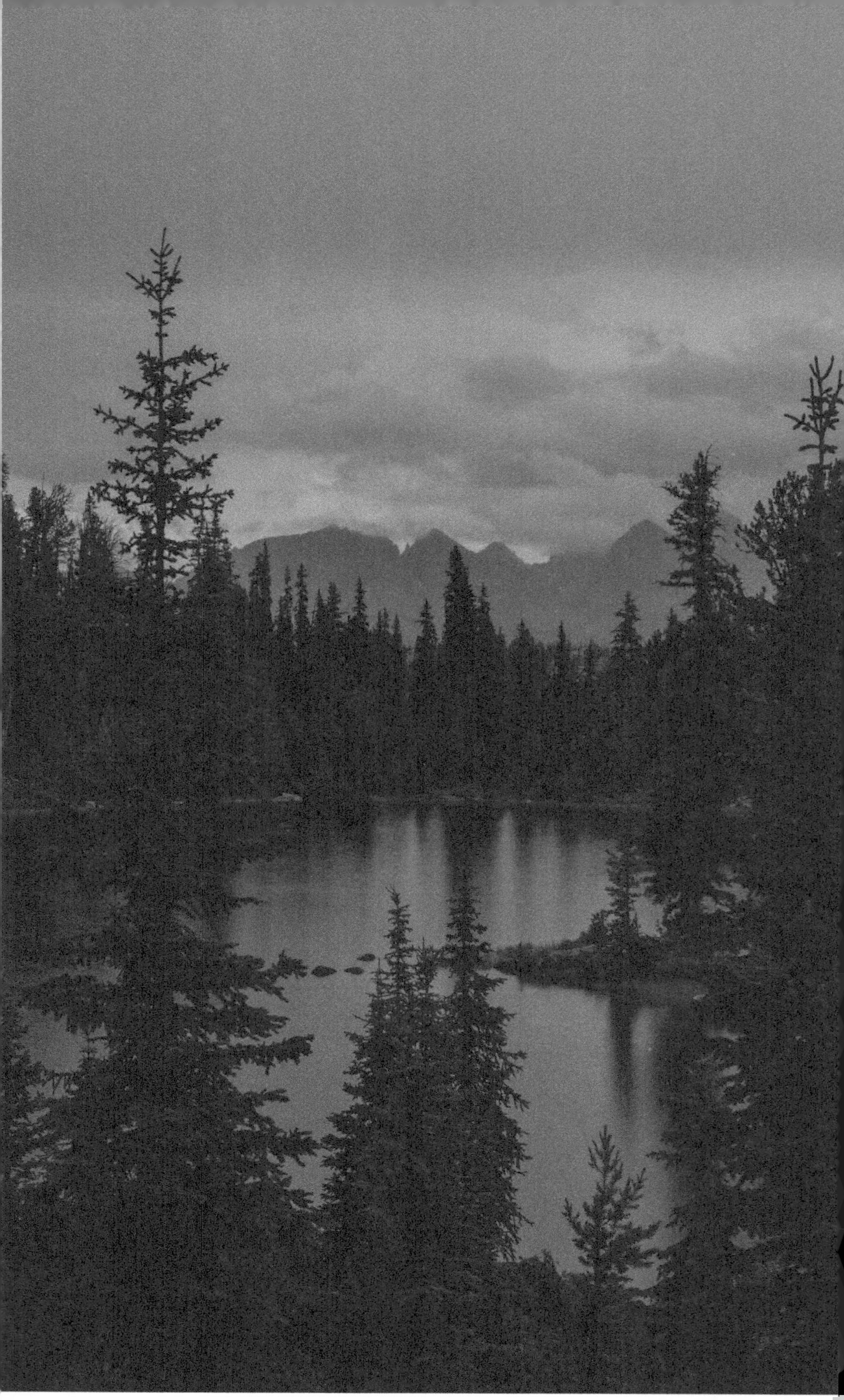

the comfort of a slow love

his soul is filled with the comfort of cloudy skies that paint the world gray.
long socks and warm mugs.
calm and pleasant.
his soul is cozy.

her soul is filled with the gentle light that streams through open windows in the morning.
fresh flowers and a well-made breakfast.
inspiring and nostalgic.
her soul is soft.

and together,
oh, my together,
they create the most exquisite existence.
content and oh so very in love.

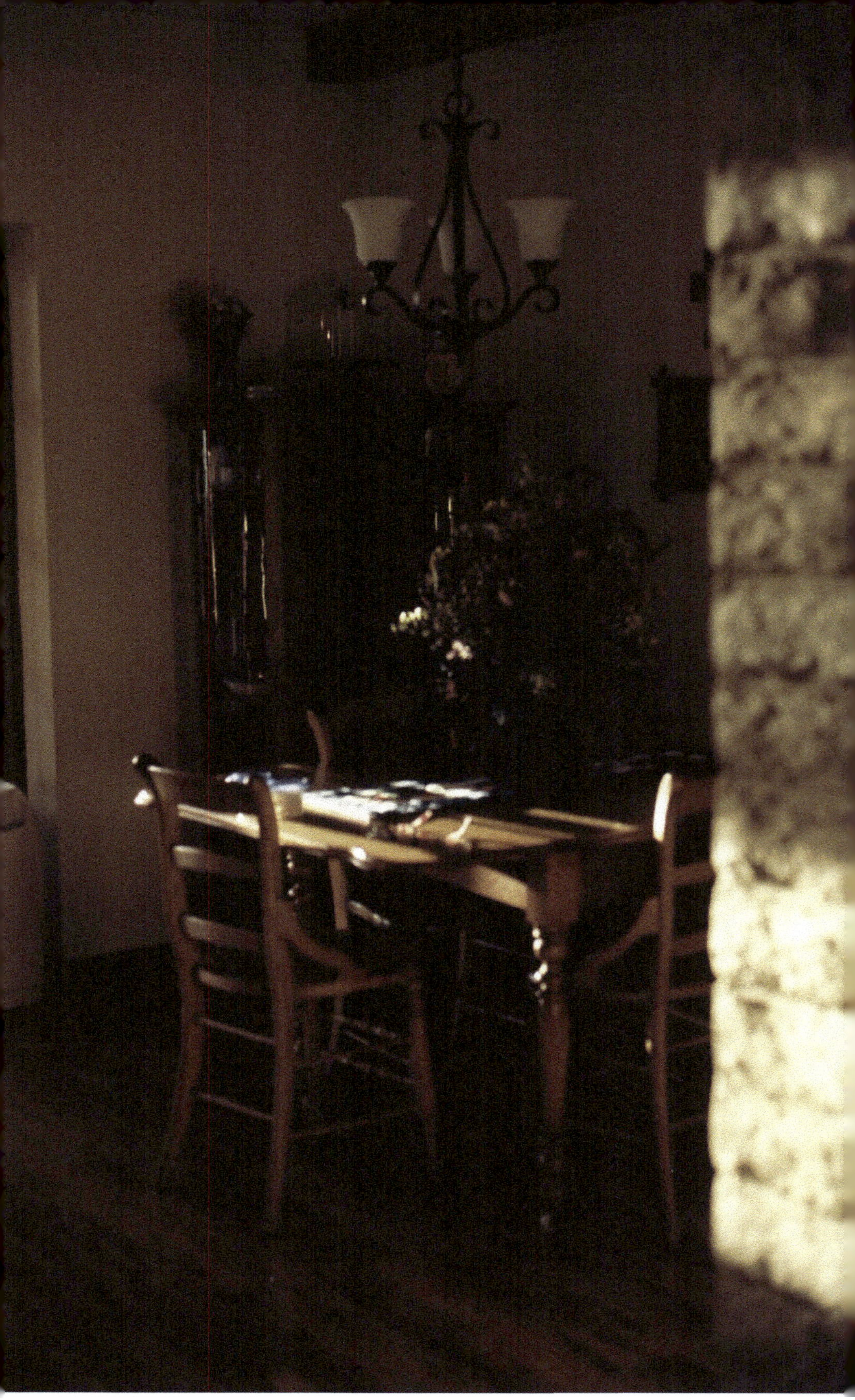

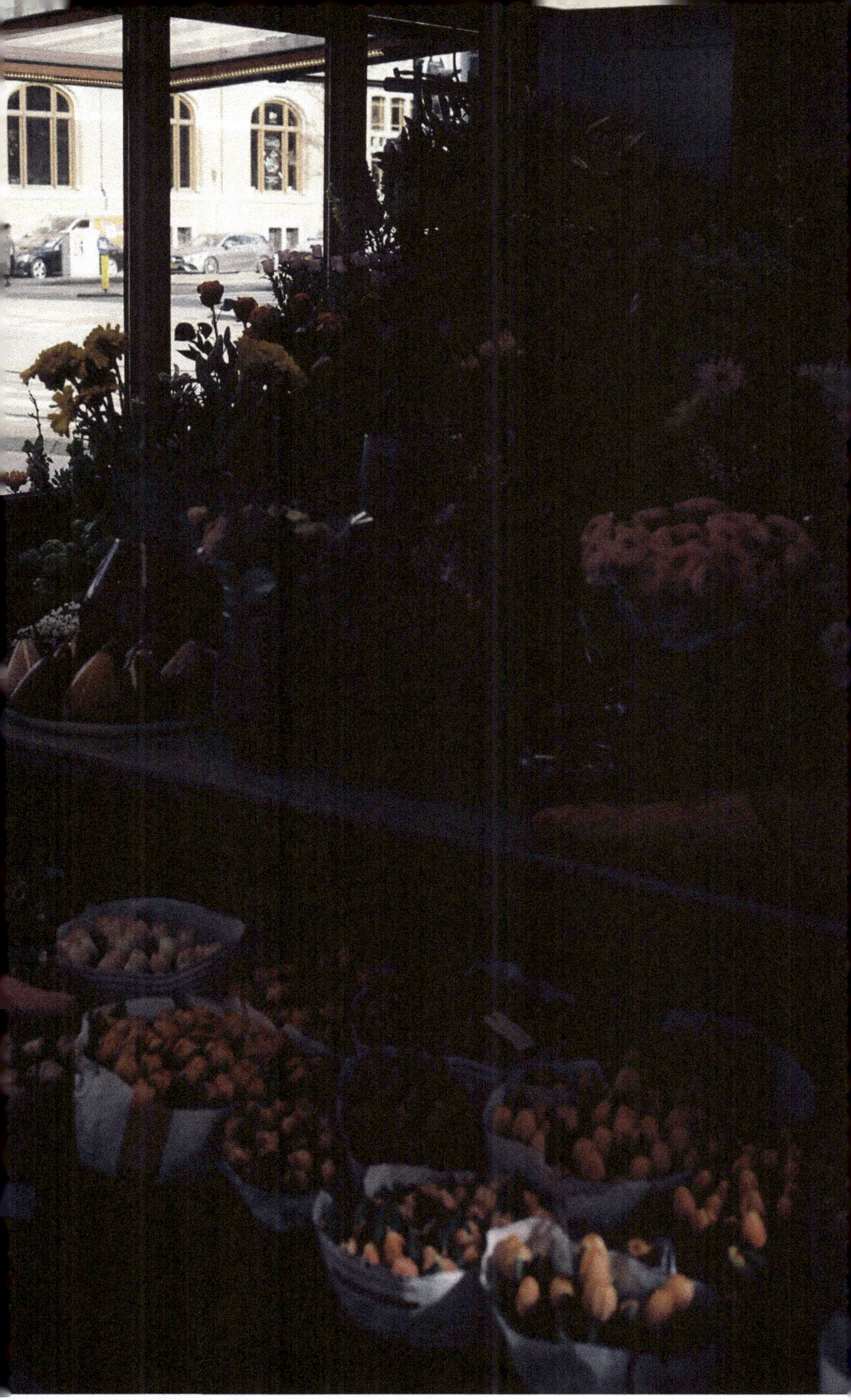

**perhaps not everyone experiences an epic love.
instead, they draw comfort in watching their beloved fall in love with life and find a home in the safety of being loved for who they are.**

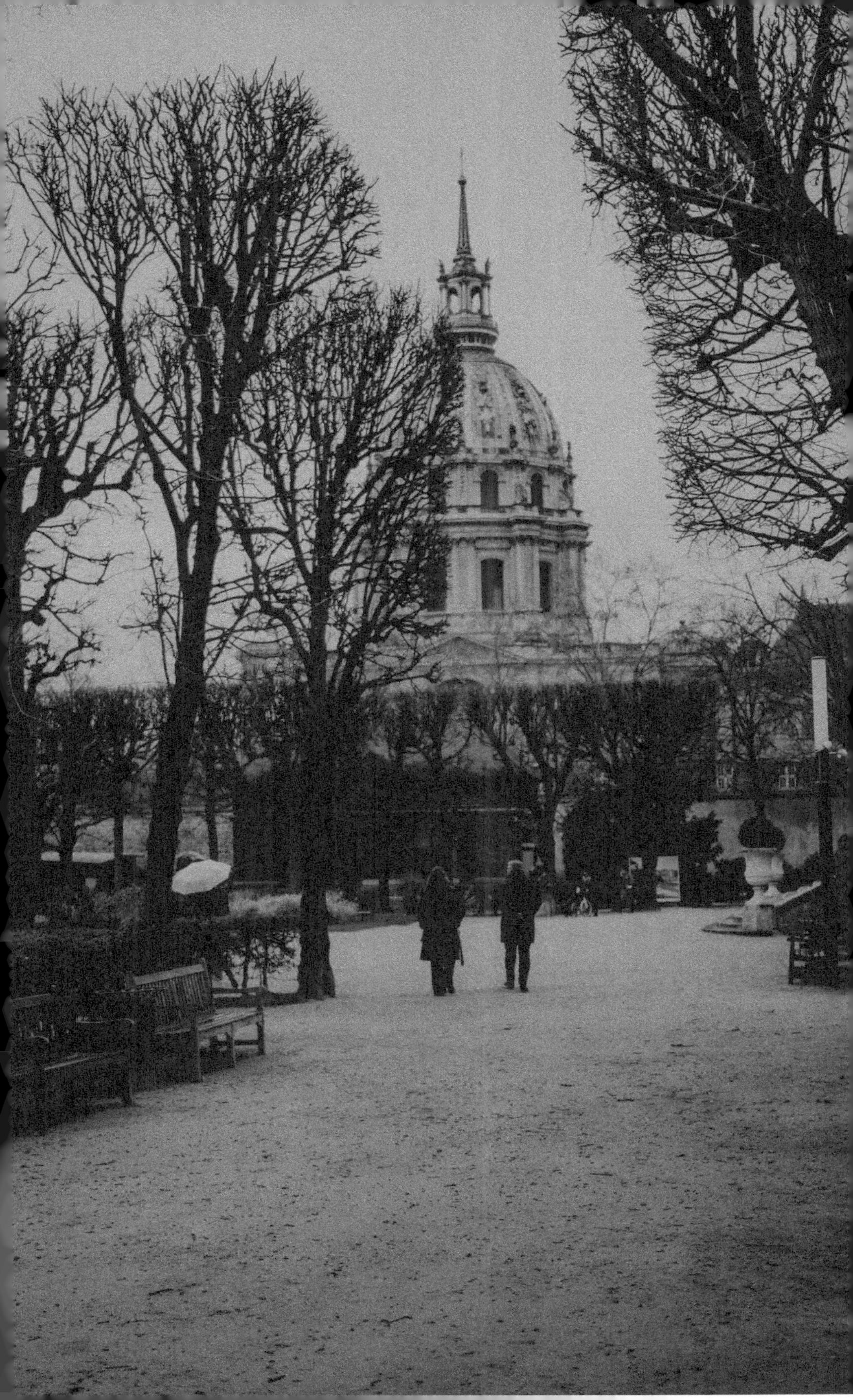

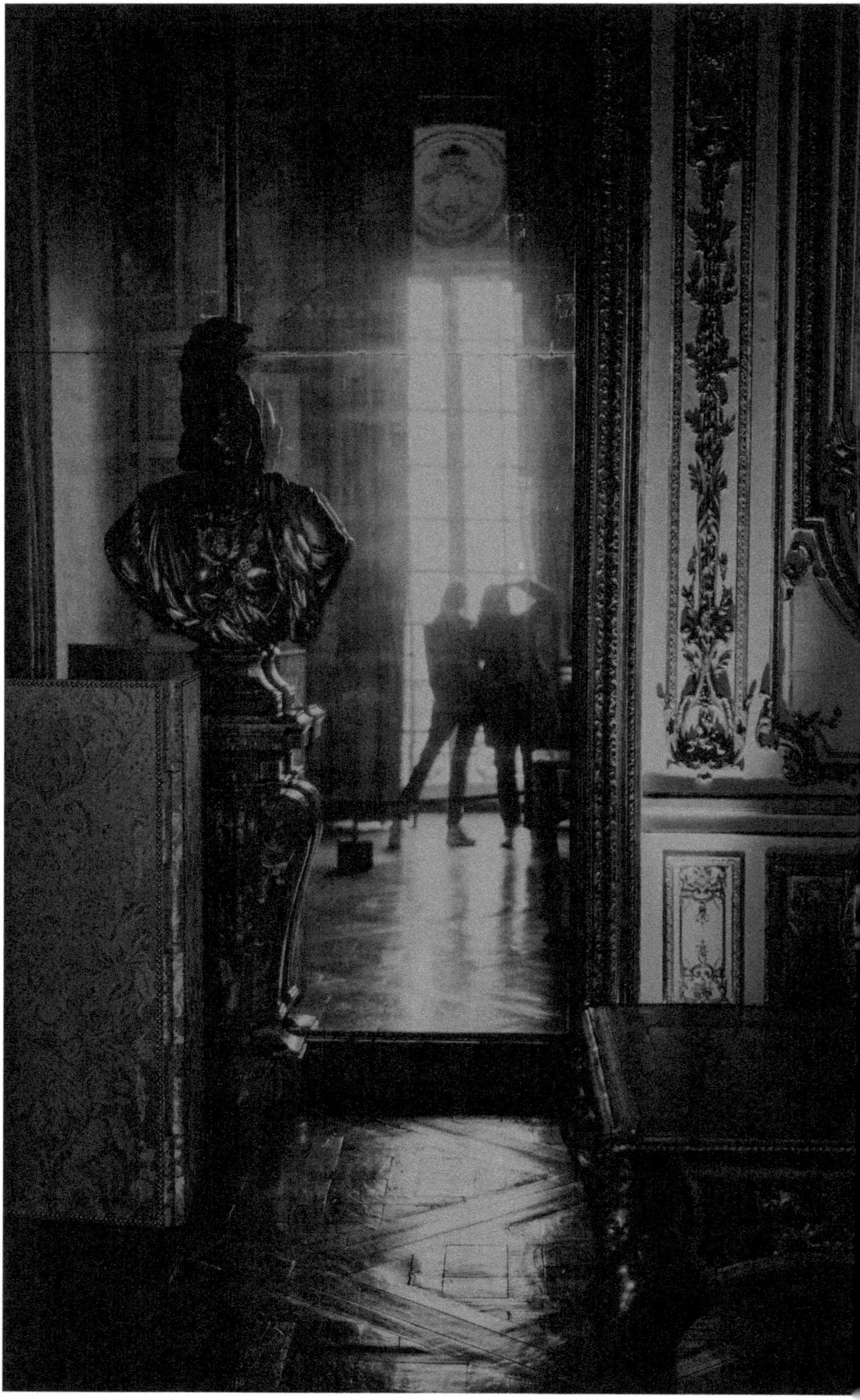

maybe home is not a place

i'm on a desperate hunt to find myself.

my heart aches for space.

i have found myself.
but in searching for my place,
i perhaps feel more lost than ever.

i am bruised and battered
and that's why i need you,
someone who is gentle with me.

a person to call home.

liquid soul

lead with your trauma.
tell me how messed up you are.
tell me the things you're afraid to say out loud.
show me your favorite playlist.
be an open book and let me turn the pages.
i want to know the thing someone said that changed you.
i want to know about the book that brought tears to your eyes.
i want to know what sets your soul on fire.
i want to know what gets you up in the morning.
i want to know your why.
don't be ashamed to let me see you cry.
forget small talk and getting to know you slowly,

pull me into your pain.
that's where love grows.

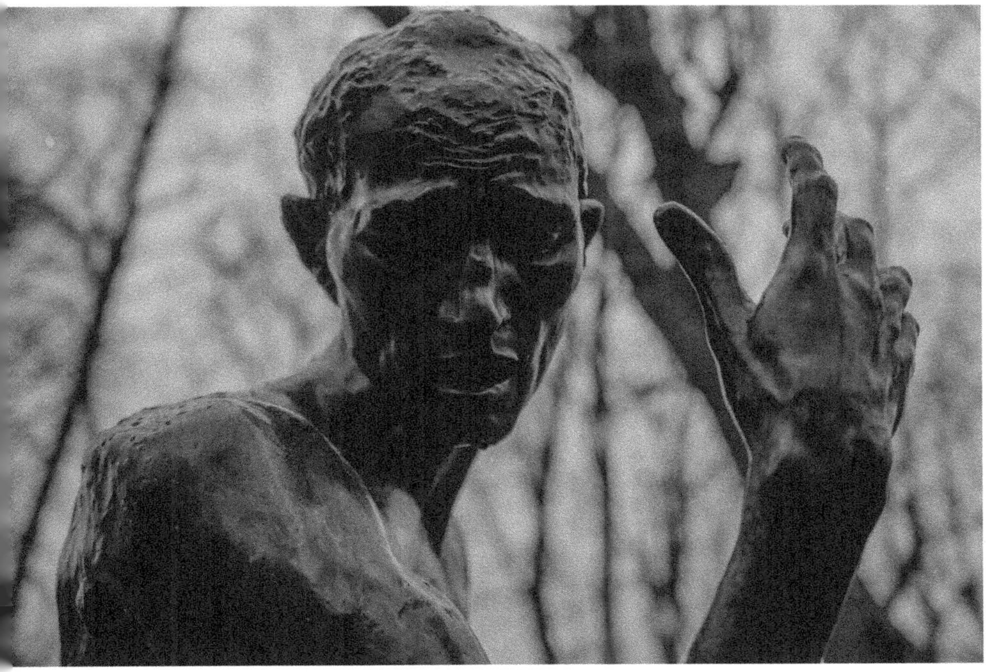

break with me

i am the owner of a broken soul.
like a mirror cracked,
reflecting in pieces,
pain pouring from all places.
running in fear from the unknown.
knowing it's easier to be alone.

a broken soul cowering,
afraid of all,
protecting itself.
fighting the wild.
yet, aching to be held like a child.

a broken soul feeling too deeply.
or choosing not to feel at all.
constantly misunderstood,
but never staying to see if someone would.
projecting their hurt onto others.
families, fathers, mothers,
friends and lovers.

a broken soul is a tattered patchwork.
tiny little fragments of self.
slivers of hope.
portions of despair.
a victim of careless wear and tear.

but we're cut from the same cloth,
you and me .
where i see pieces,
you see me.
tarnished and rough,
but you thought i was enough.
the shards of soul scattered and confused,
used and abused,

slowly finding their way

together.
no longer forced to run.
ceasing to roam.
in you, this broken soul has found a home.

perhaps in its essence life
is unbearable
and that's why we believe
in love.

thoughts i had while lying in your arms

sometimes moments of life are so
rich you just want to soak it all in.
remember the smells,
the texture of existence,
the beautiful aching sadness of
only living once.
for a moment, it's more than just
ok.

happiness lives in these spaces.

hold it.

clutch onto it.

it's these tiny pockets of peace that
make life worth living.

a mirrorless reflection

there is something to be said for the
simple intimacy of being understood.
easily, just as you are.
uncompromising.

unwavering.

unafraid.

the freedom to exist as you have always
wanted to.
when things fall into place and words
do not just hang in space.
that is where we found ourselves.
no longer forced to explain or beg for
understanding,
nestled softly in the comfort of
uncomplicated conversation.

i was scattered and messy,
like an orchestra warming up.
you tightened my strings.
set me upright.
took me from the dark and put me in
the light.
a beautiful difference you made.
oh, the music we played.

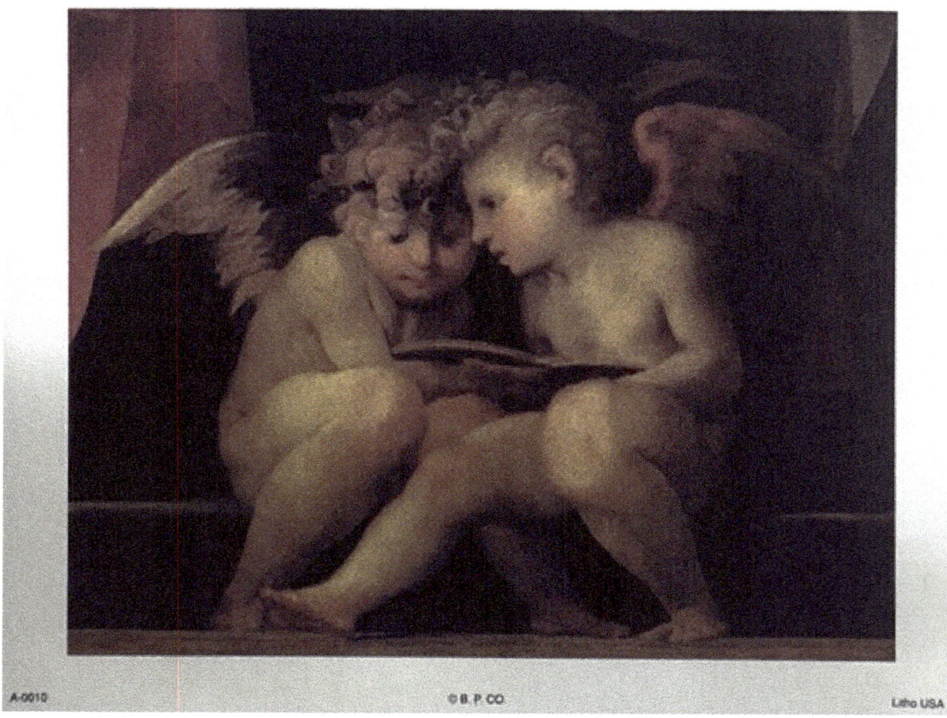

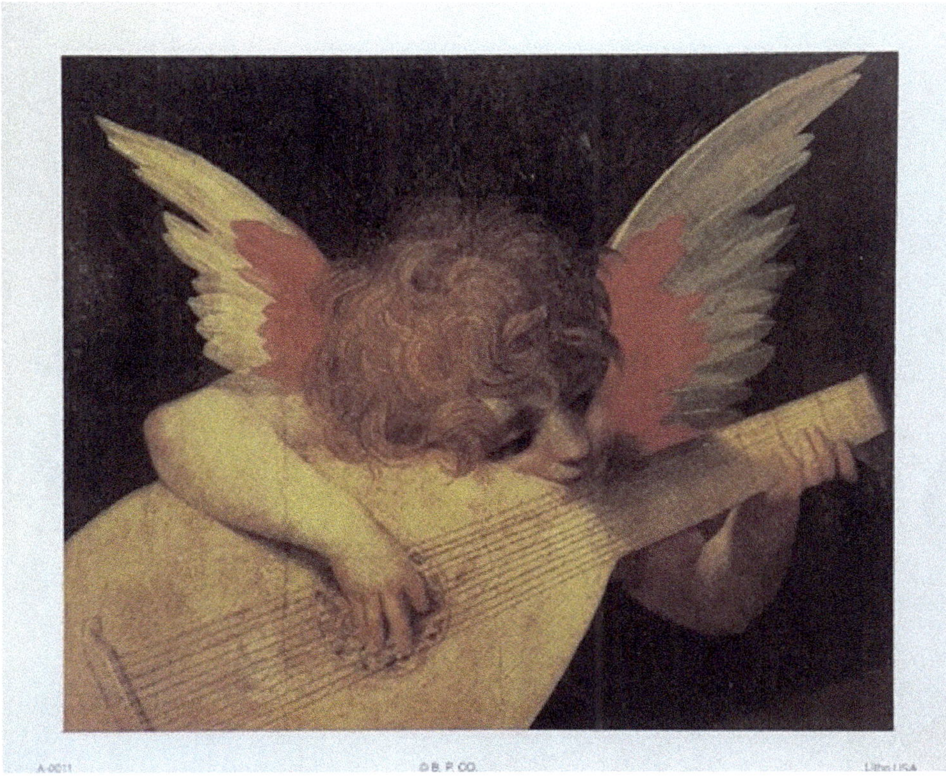

in the soundtrack of my life,
you were my favorite note.
even if played ever so briefly.

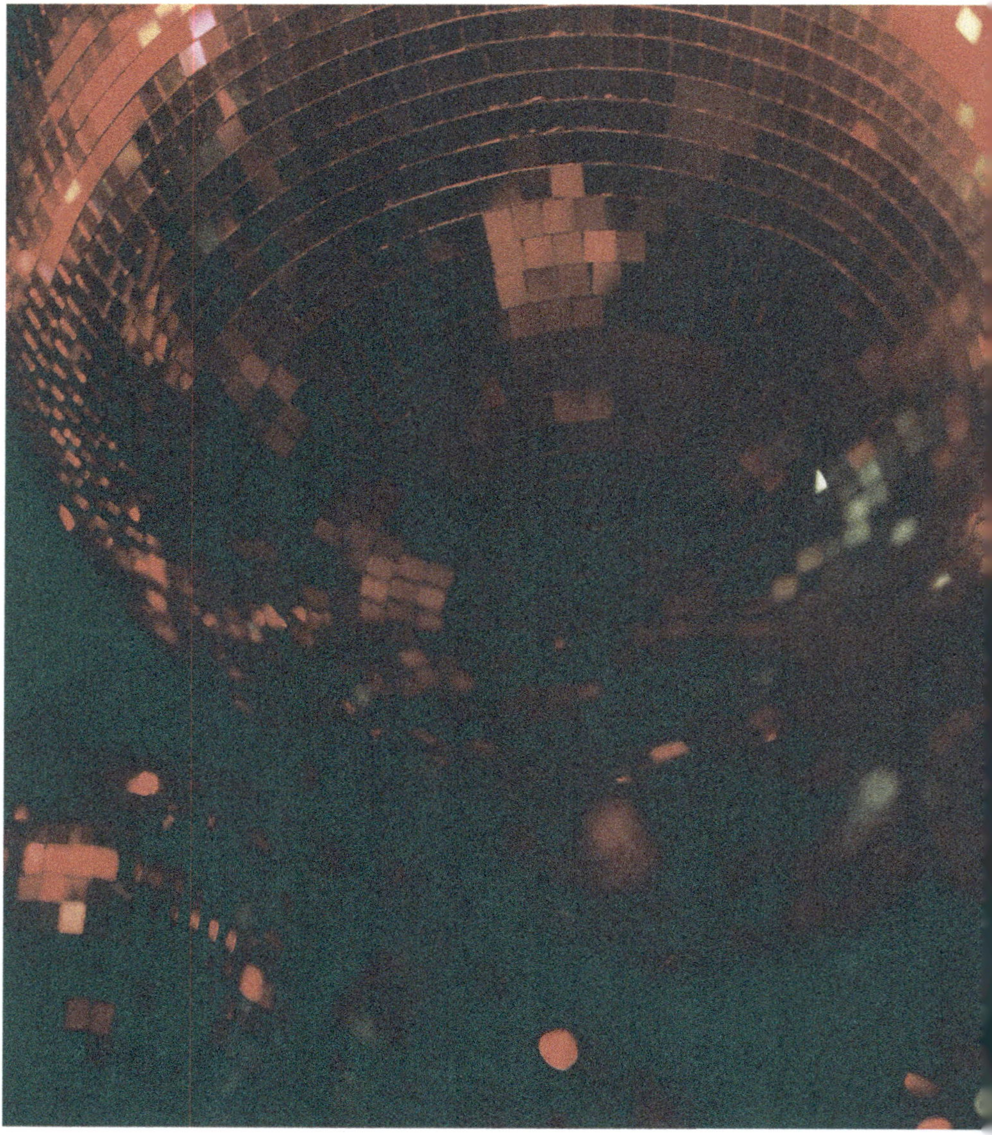

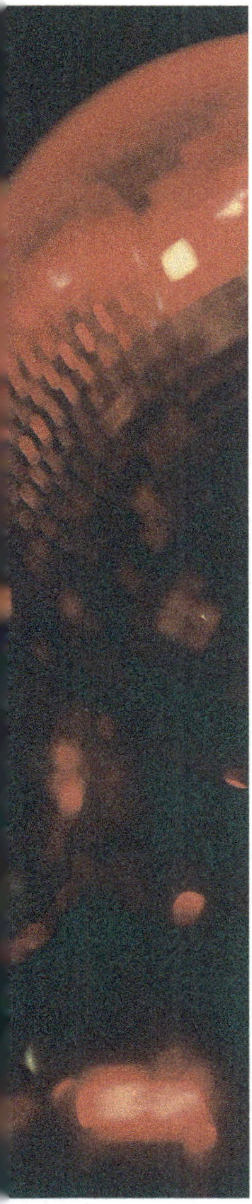

my first friday night without you

i leave the party early,
just to feel sad on the way home.

i don't wanna be there.
but i don't want to be alone.

you would have made me stay,
making eye contact through the crowd.

us.
our little secret never said out loud.

i can see you smiling as i shyly watched,
siping the drink in my hand but intoxicated by you.

spending the night dreaming, waiting,
for the clutches that encompass being just us two.

you, the life of the party,
the one everyone wanted to be around.

then in a moment,
gone from my life without as a sound.

my heart ripped from my chest,
the pain the only thing that is true.

so i'll sit through this green light just thinking of you,
maybe becasue i miss you, or maybe becasue i don't
know

what else to do.

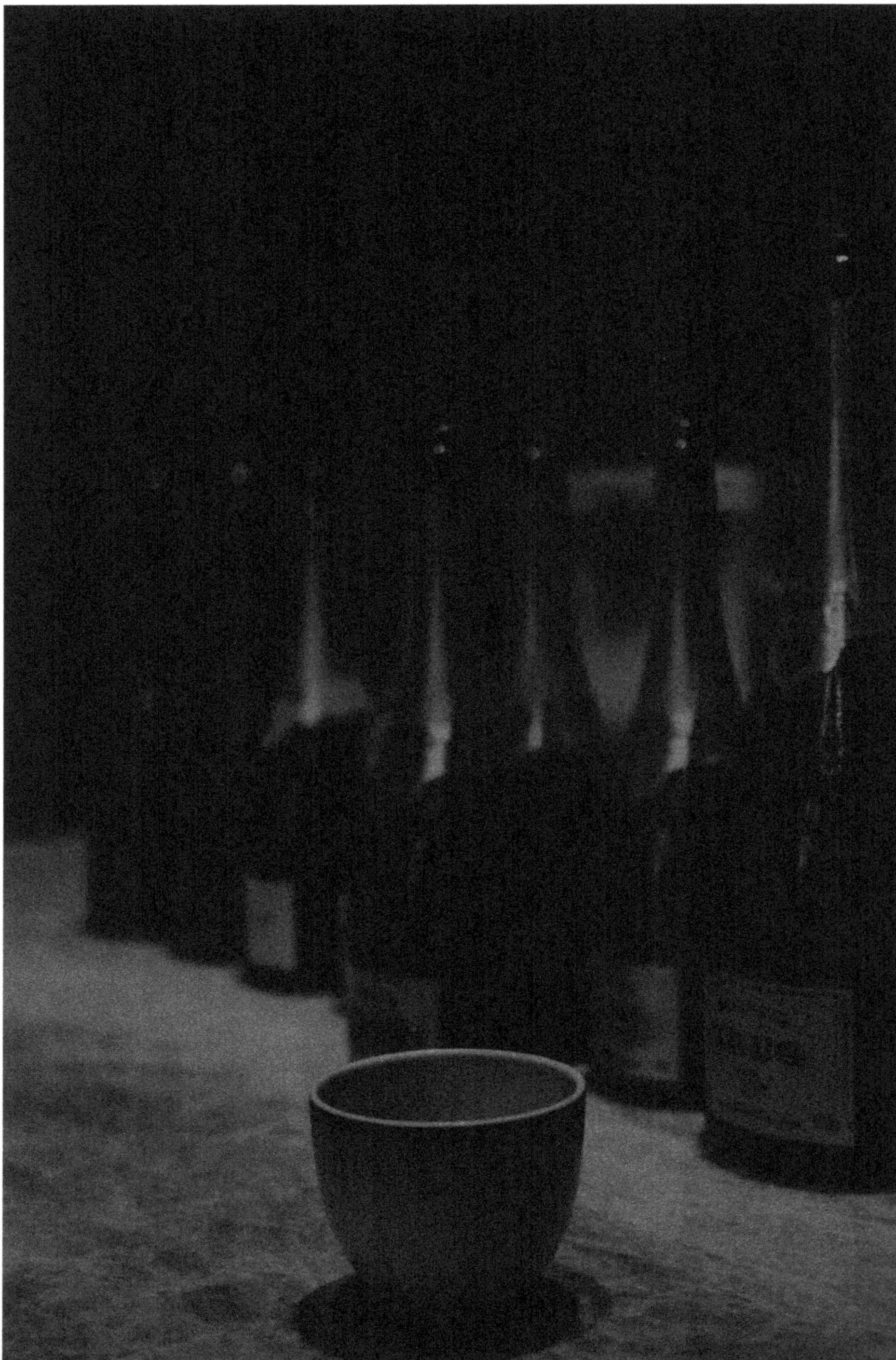

when the inhibition became low and drunk words spoke of sober
thoughts, that's where we found our us,
dancing on the edge of disaster.

i just wanted to hear your voice.
to drown the deafening volume of my own.

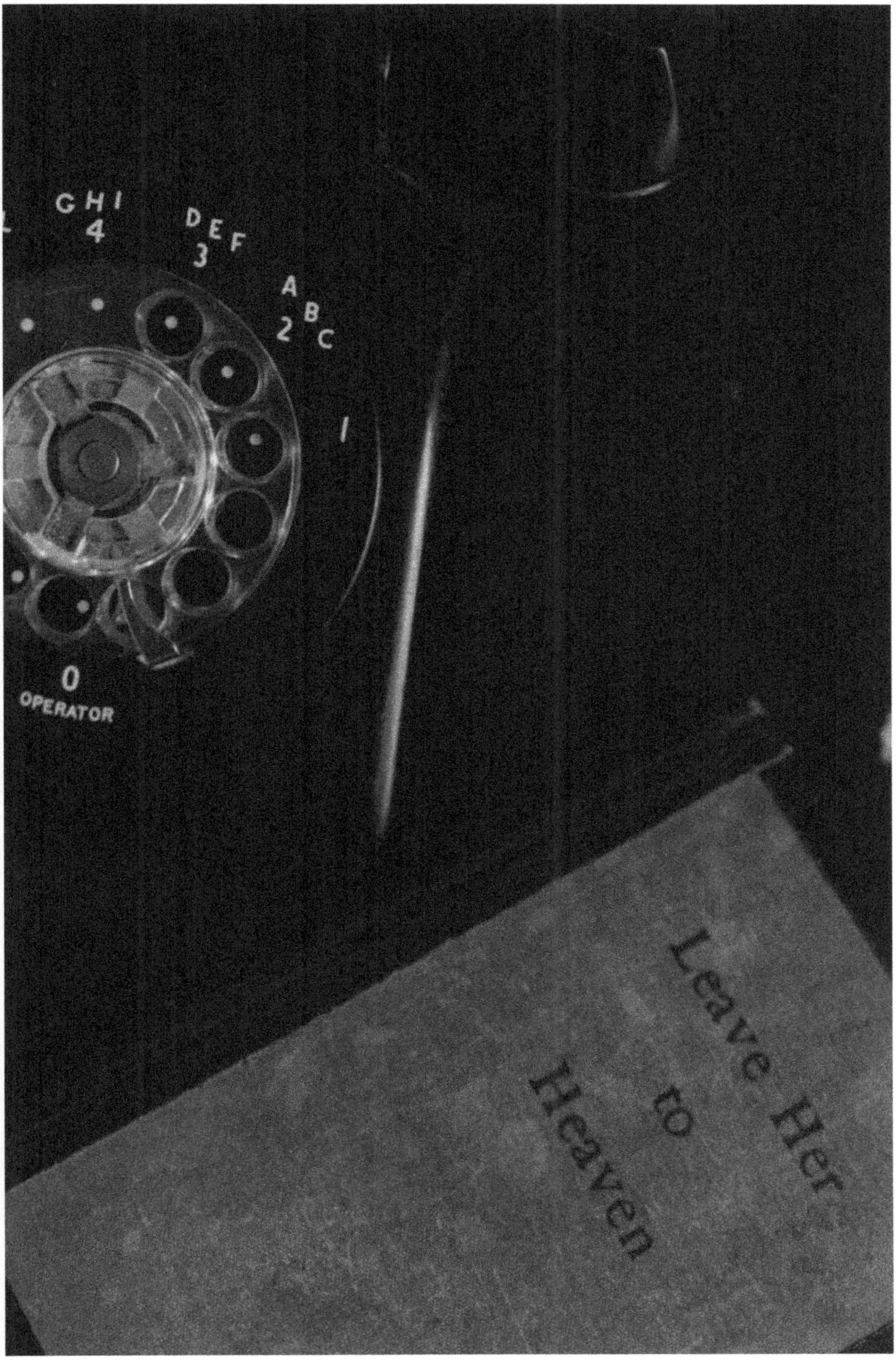

maybe that's why you

captivated me so wholly,

because for the first time in a

long time, i felt wanted,

and you wanted me so badly it

consumed you.

a heat damned to burn itself out.

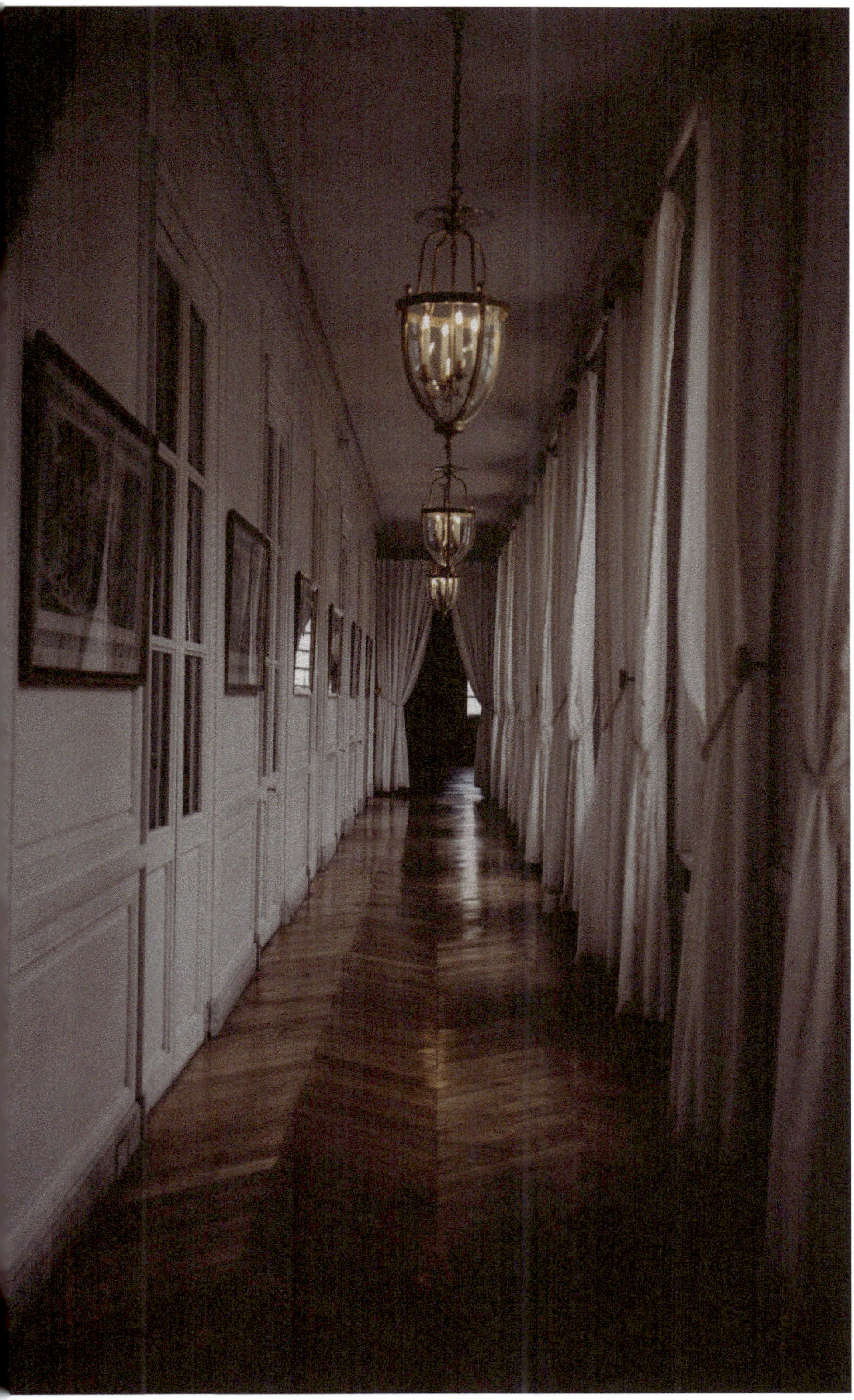

THE REAL PARTY
STARTS WHEN
EVERYONE LEAVE

♡ KADE

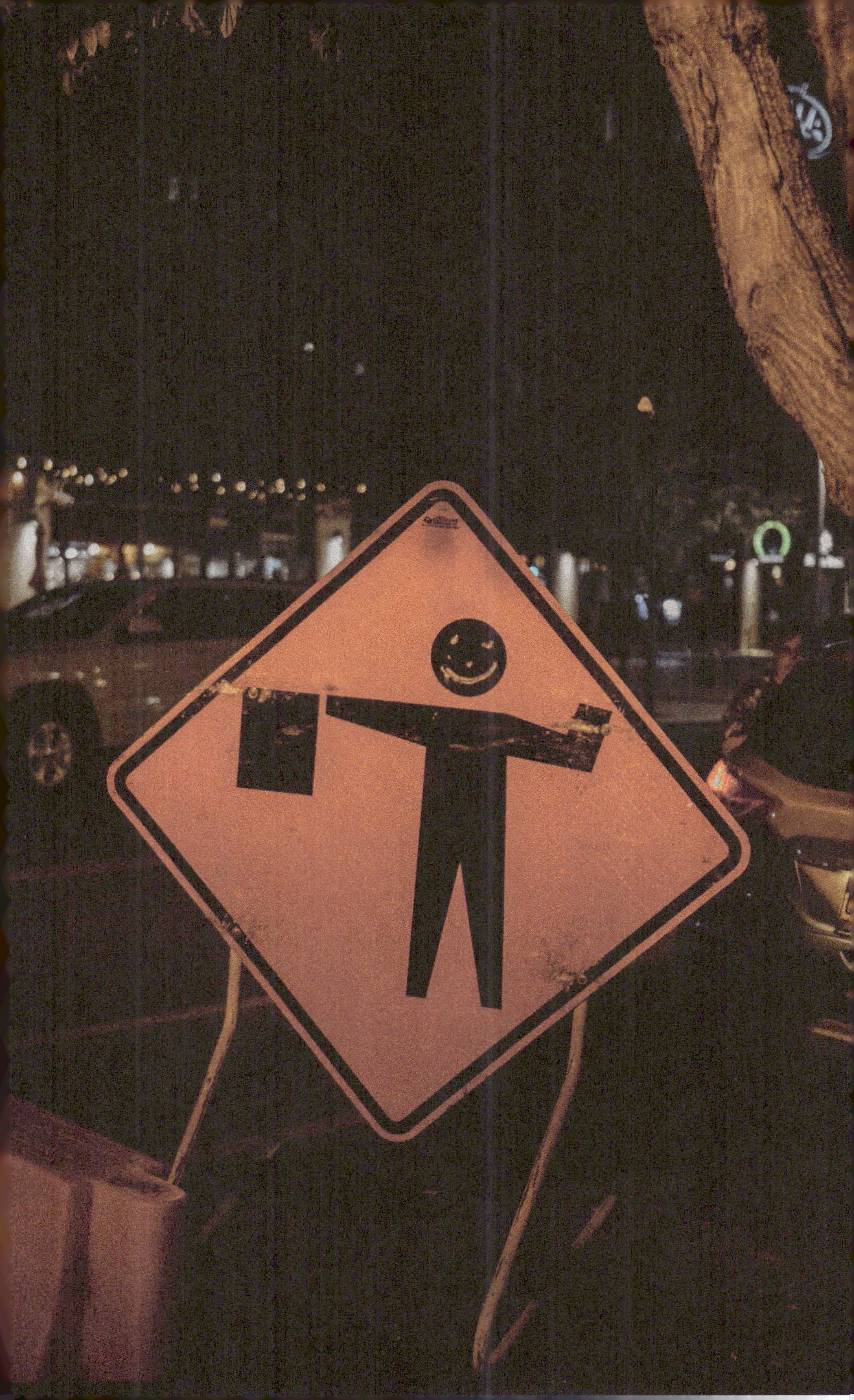

maybe i said too much... maybe i didn't say enough

i feel like i'm just spinning,
and making little progress.
overly aware of myself and the space i am taking.
wishing i could shrink,

out of existence,

out of everyone's mind,

out of my own.

simultaneously wanting to be seen and understood,
and never wanting to be noticed again.

i guess i just wish you were here.

just tell me its ok.

please, tell me its ok.

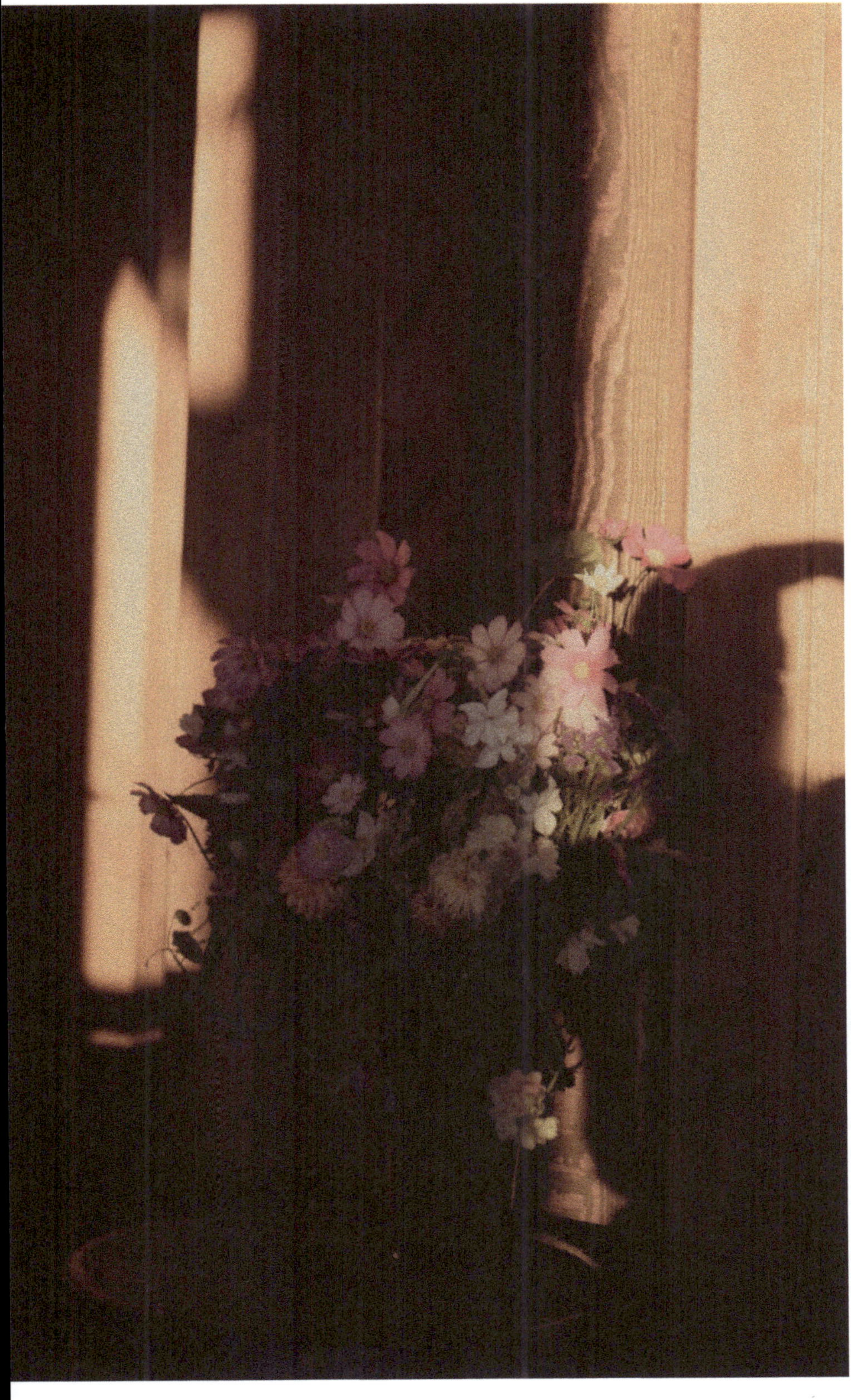

i used to know your kiss, but now it's foreign to me,
in every brush of our lips lingers the taste of misery.

icarus

i grew wings.
i learned to fly.
i shook off all that held me back.
threw myself, unafraid, into the blue sky.

i experienced ecstasy.
i tasted freedom, but no more.
my wings were clipped.
instantly revoking my ability to soar.

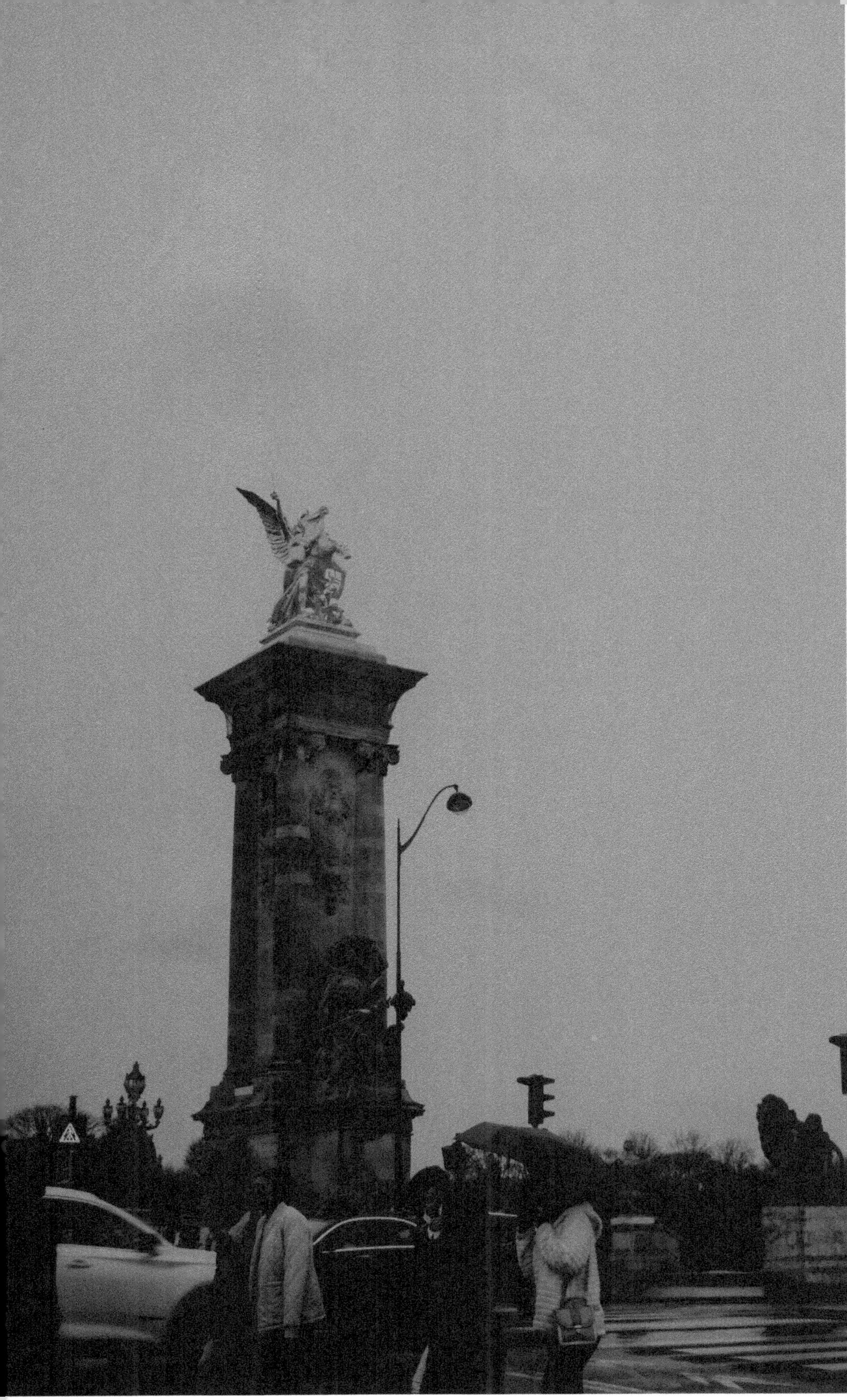

to the death of a dream

it's hard to watch the winds of life blow away the sands of hope.
to witness something, clutched onto with the entirety of your being, turn to dust in your grasp.
perhaps time is truly the most painful thing of all, because it is the only thing that lasts.

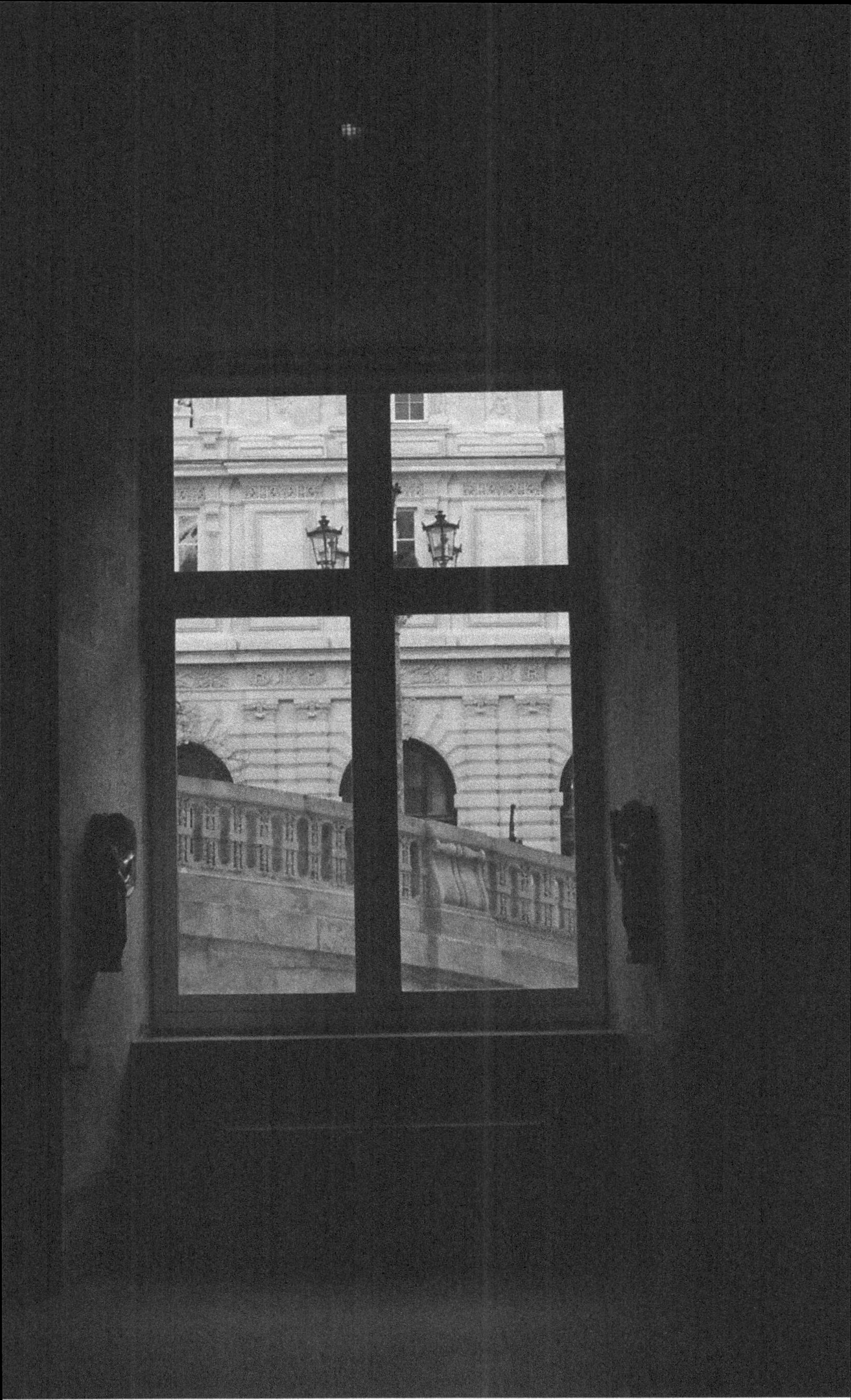

glass bubble bath

you pulled the plug,
drained me dry,
willing yourself to make me cry.

you took all i had to give,
and begged for more,
leaving my body bruised and sore.

you left me to drown,
in a bath of my own fool.
aching to see the good, ignoring your cruel.

you laughed at my sputtering,
shoving me down,
shattering my bent and battered crown.

i just wanted to breathe,
inhale and exhale at my own speed,
but the pain you thirsted for was a need.

did it make you feel powerful. . .
to break a broken girl?

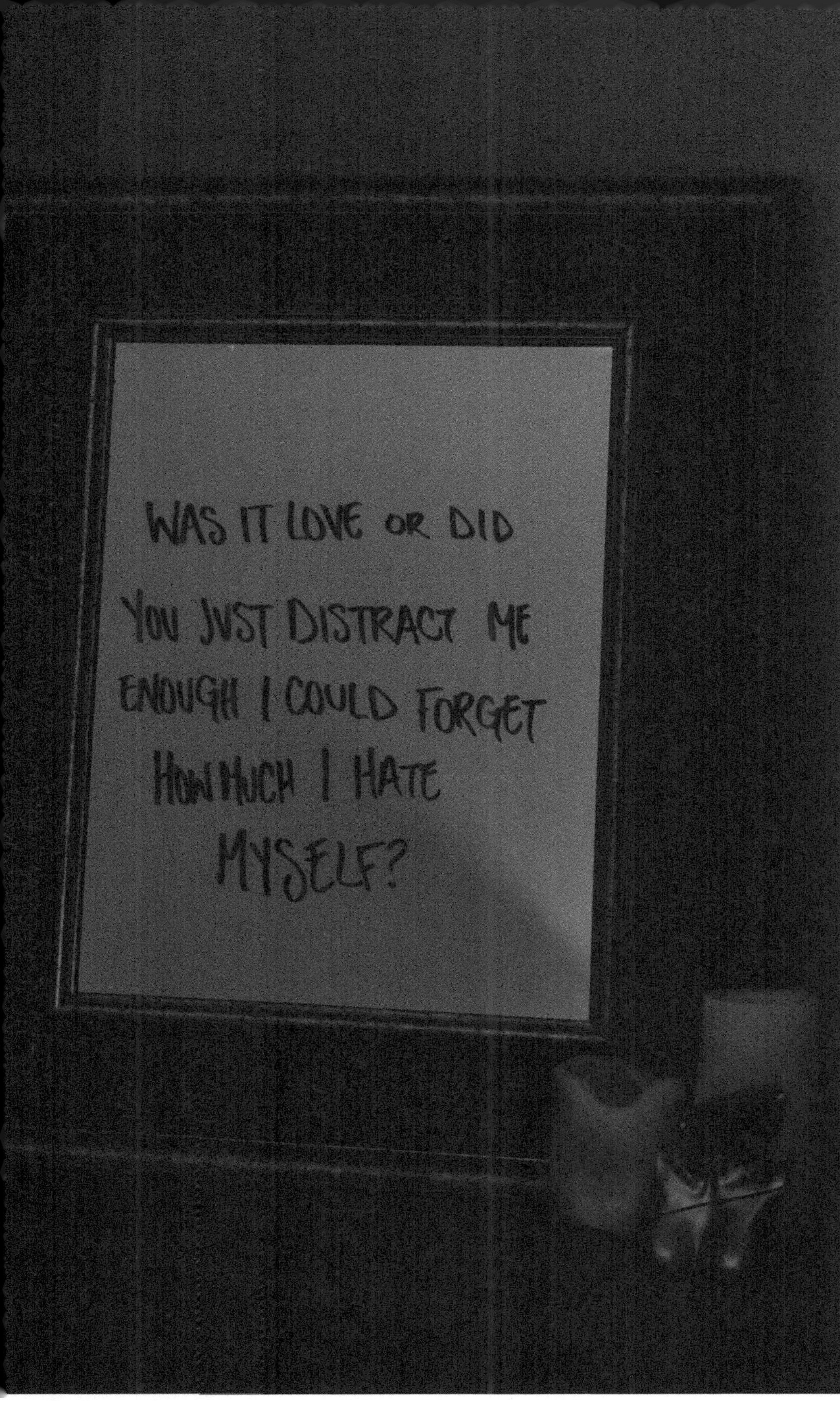
WAS IT LOVE OR DID
YOU JUST DISTRACT ME
ENOUGH I COULD FORGET
HOW MUCH I HATE
MYSELF?

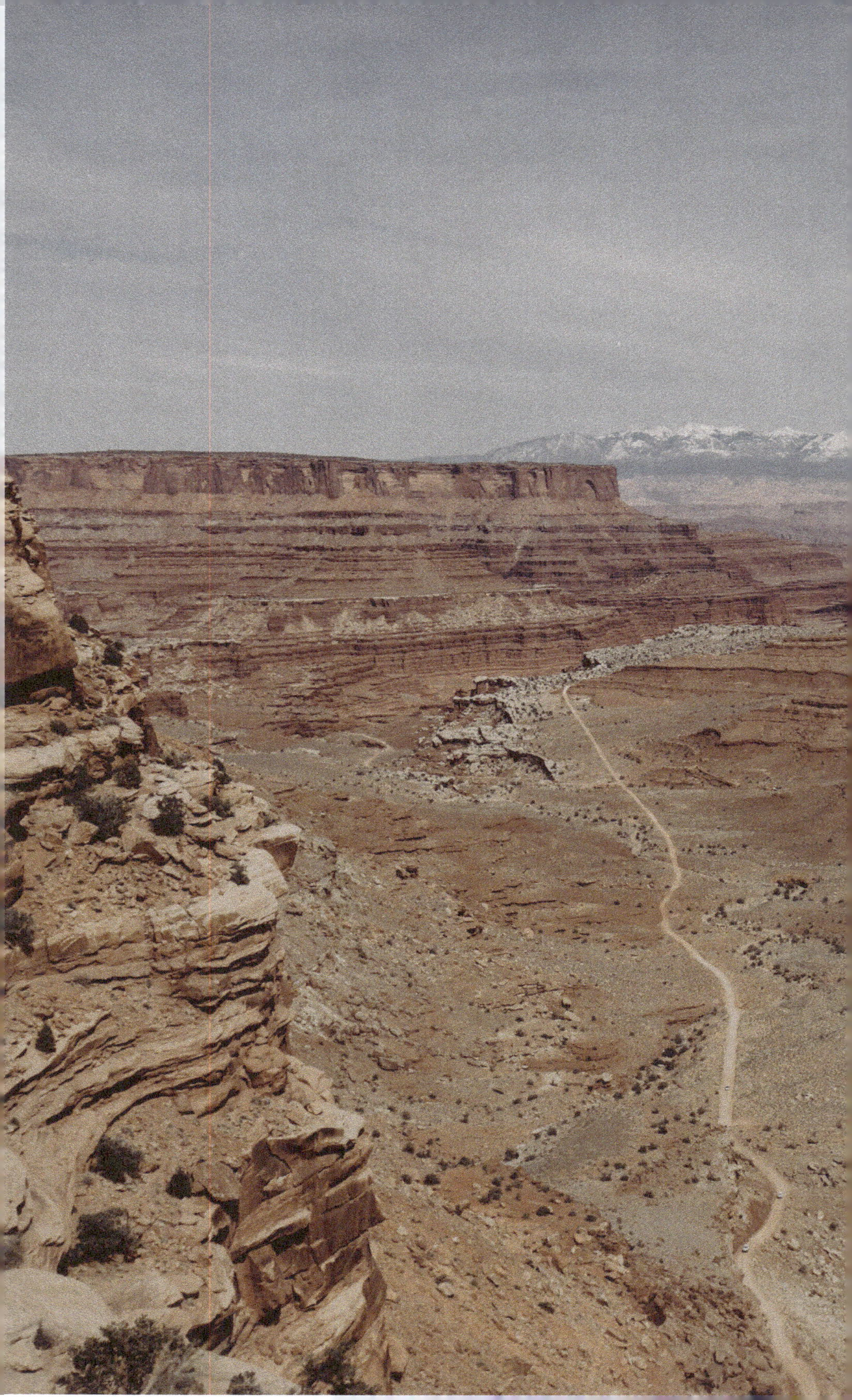

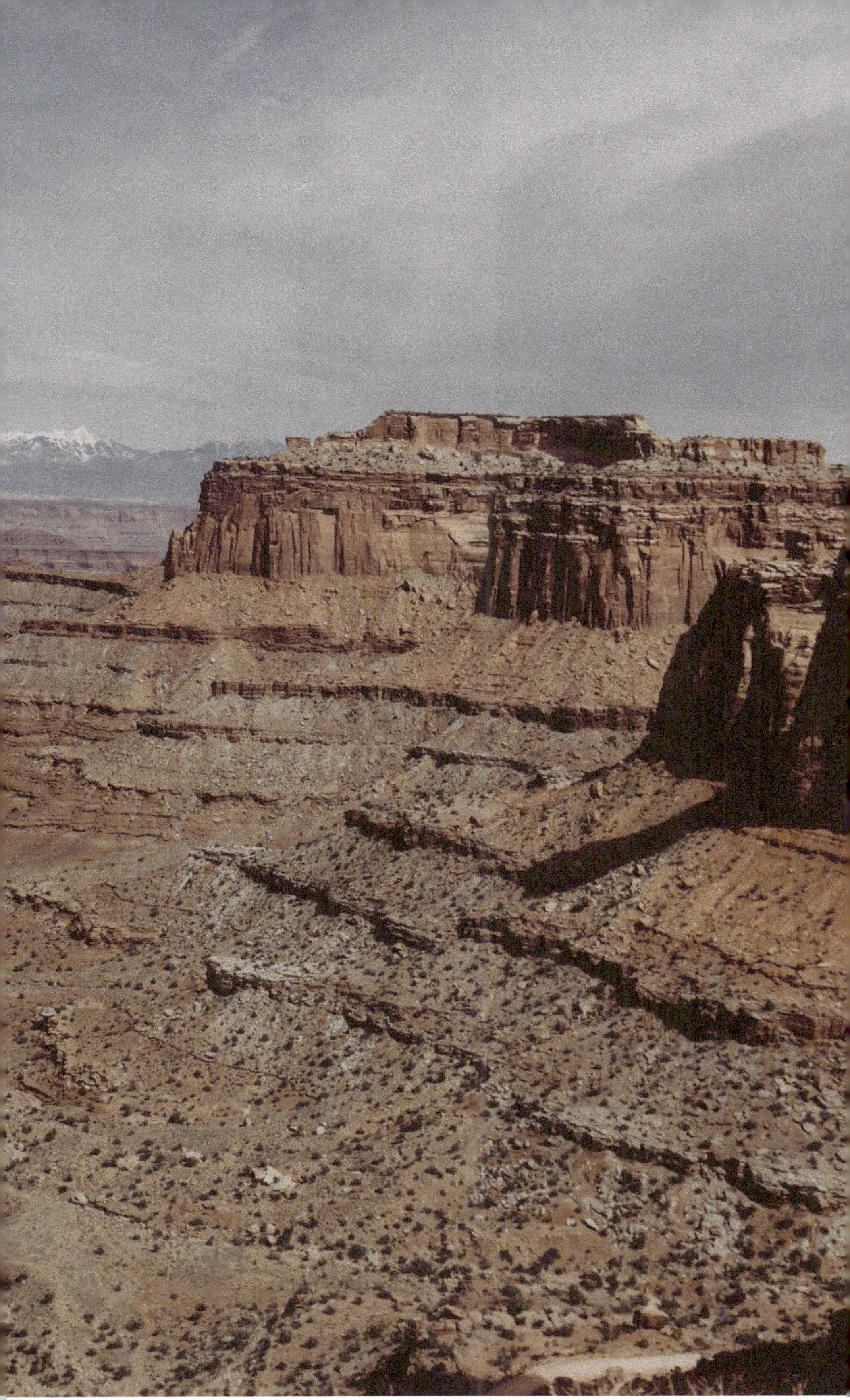

go sit in the corner and think about what you did

you told me you loved me.

you lied.

true love would damn your selfish pride.

you slandered my name without a care.

only a fool would see love there.

a man in love would rather die,

than see tears pour from their lover's eye,

and you laughed at the torrents pouring out of mine.

told me to shut up,

it was my fault,

i was fine.

you said i broke down every wall you had built,

yet you kept my name in the lies you spilt.

that's not love.

you played my open heart like an experiment.

you are an embarrassment,

that's betrayal to a heart i put in your hand.

so, was it not real love or are you just not a man?

shadow self

you wanted to see me, to dive into my depths,
but you were mad i only gave you my shadow self.
you wanted something to grasp, something to hold, a being to control.
i gave you my shadow to see how you would react,
a secret i kept to hold myself intact.
you thought i was cheating you, not giving you myself,
thought i was holding back, putting you on a shelf,
so you demanded more.

but, i gave you my shadow because she is me,
existing in a plaguing duality.
she is the me i cannot control.
she stretches in the light, hides in the shade,
an unrefined, unmade, raw outline of me.
i think she holds my soul. that's why you can't find it.
she's creative, wild, free and untamed.
she has never left my side despite being unnamed.
she laughs when i laugh and shakes when i cry,
she effortlessly exists, the sole piece of me that doesn't try.

yet, perhaps that's why you didn't want her,
you saw an outline, pleasing in form, but evading your grasp.
and when she moved, you didn't like the changing versions of me,
a black muddled mess, uncontrolled in this reality.
you just wanted the form of me,
something you could feel, touch, and see.
so you blocked out the sun, tried to make yourself my sky,
darkened my days, left my shadow self alone to cry.
you didn't want me, messy and unrestrained,
you only wanted the version of me that could be broken and drained.

but that's the beauty of my shadow self,
she's a part of me here to stay.
my spirit, my soul, my lifelong companion,
myself and the sun are the only ones who can change her,
a shadow i'm thankful is immune to your sway.
and when you left and took your dark sky with you,
you thought you left only a shadow of the woman you knew,
you thought you took us all, every piece, a life cut through.
but how wrong you are.
it would be easier to capture a star.
my shadow is resistant to scars.

predator.

sometimes he looks at me in a certain way, with a devious glint in his eye. studying me as one does a textbook, raking in what scraps of me he can grasp onto. and i will find myself squirming, trapped under his predatory gaze. over examining the stem of my glass. making mental notes on the way the moonlight reflects in the white tones of my wine. anything to avoid staring back into his eyes. for he looks at me as though he wants to consume me. not in a romantic, sweet intoxicating scent of summer love kind of consumption. but in the way a match looks at a candle, eager to burn it to the ground. killing it simply for its scent. my aroma of innocence
entices him, a youth he can clutch onto. a twisted past able to be expunged in the pungent odor of unknowing perspective. he listens to me. holds onto every word i say, knowing i love to be heard. but, i know behind his steady look whir the twisted cogs of desire. he whispers to me of how interesting i am. how different. how unique. he slathers on charm. disarms me with his directness. piecing me together, saying what i want to hear.

"i like that you underline in books."

"you're different."

"you stubborn, difficult child."

he perhaps expects me to be falling for it...
this broken game of cat and mouse. but i see into his eyes and peek into his blackened soul. wrestling with himself. lulling me into a sense of security so he can remove his own guilt when he poaches his prize. he knows he can win. a trained hunter.
however, i shall remain an elusive prey. for my gut, who has never wronged me, sits inside of me steeped in discernment, and whispers, "run."

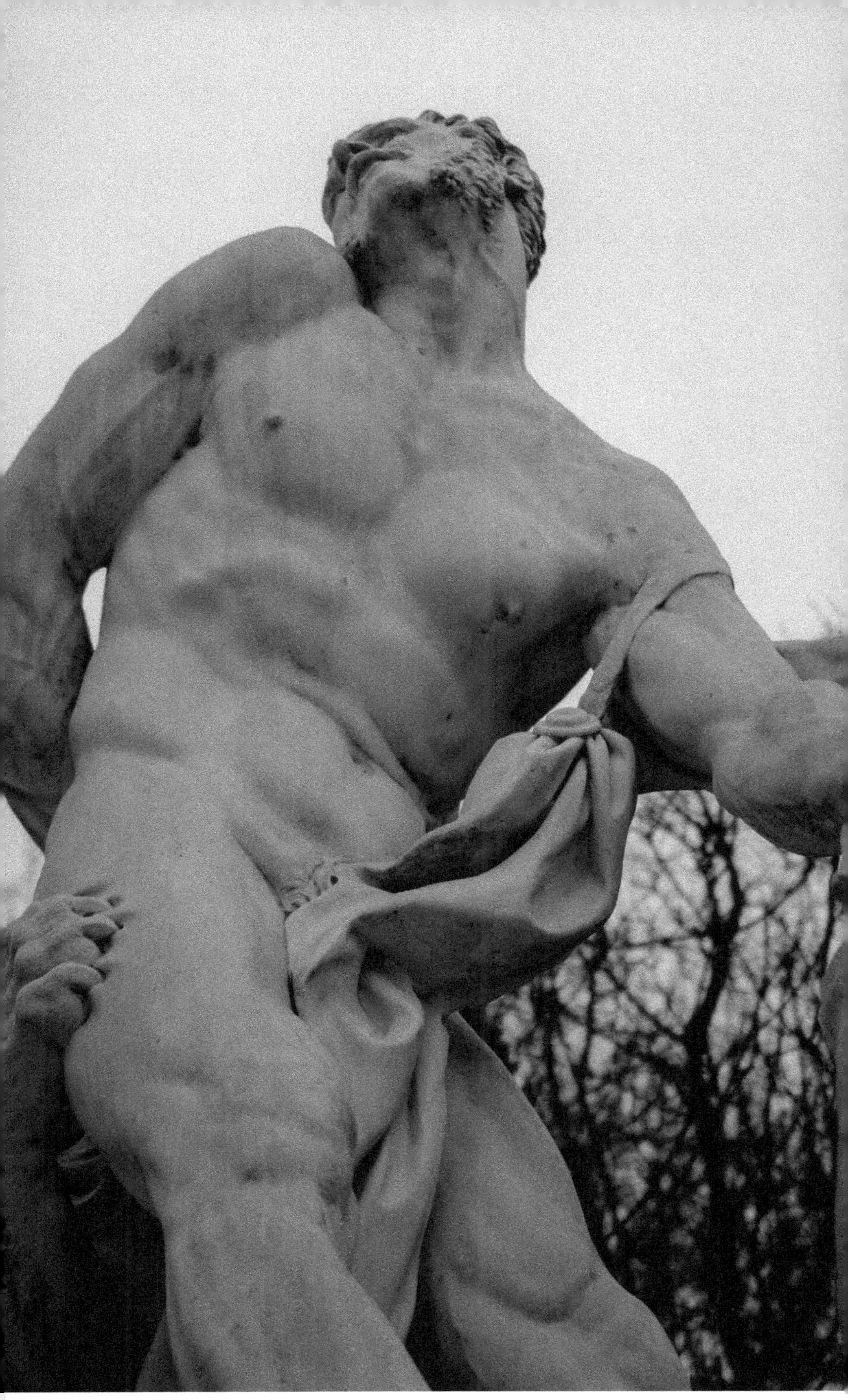

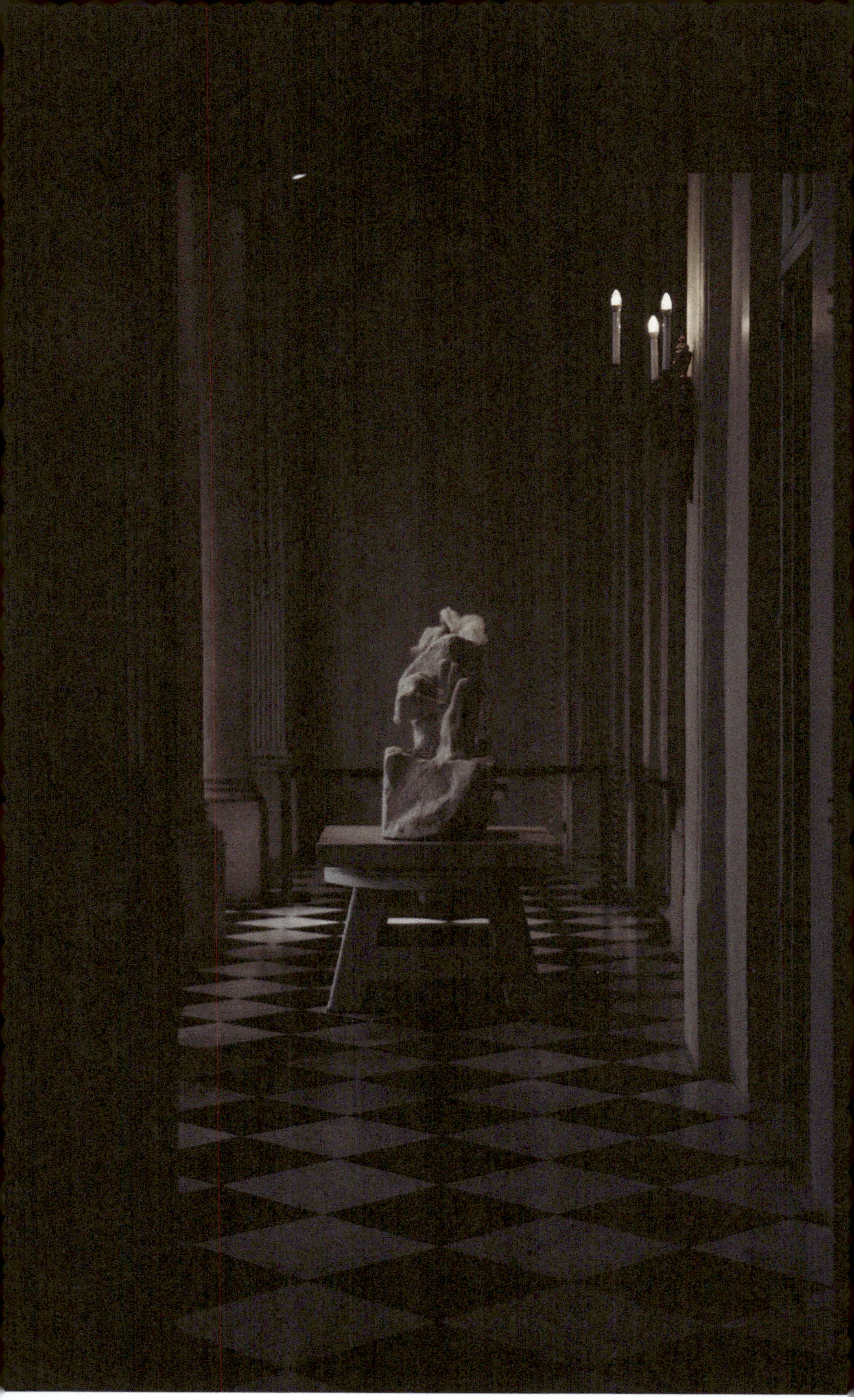

sometimes i look through old photos just to break my own heart over again.
i don't know why, or perhaps i don't want to admit i do.
it's simply because memories are all i have left of you.

beware of baring your body with those to whom you would not bare your soul.

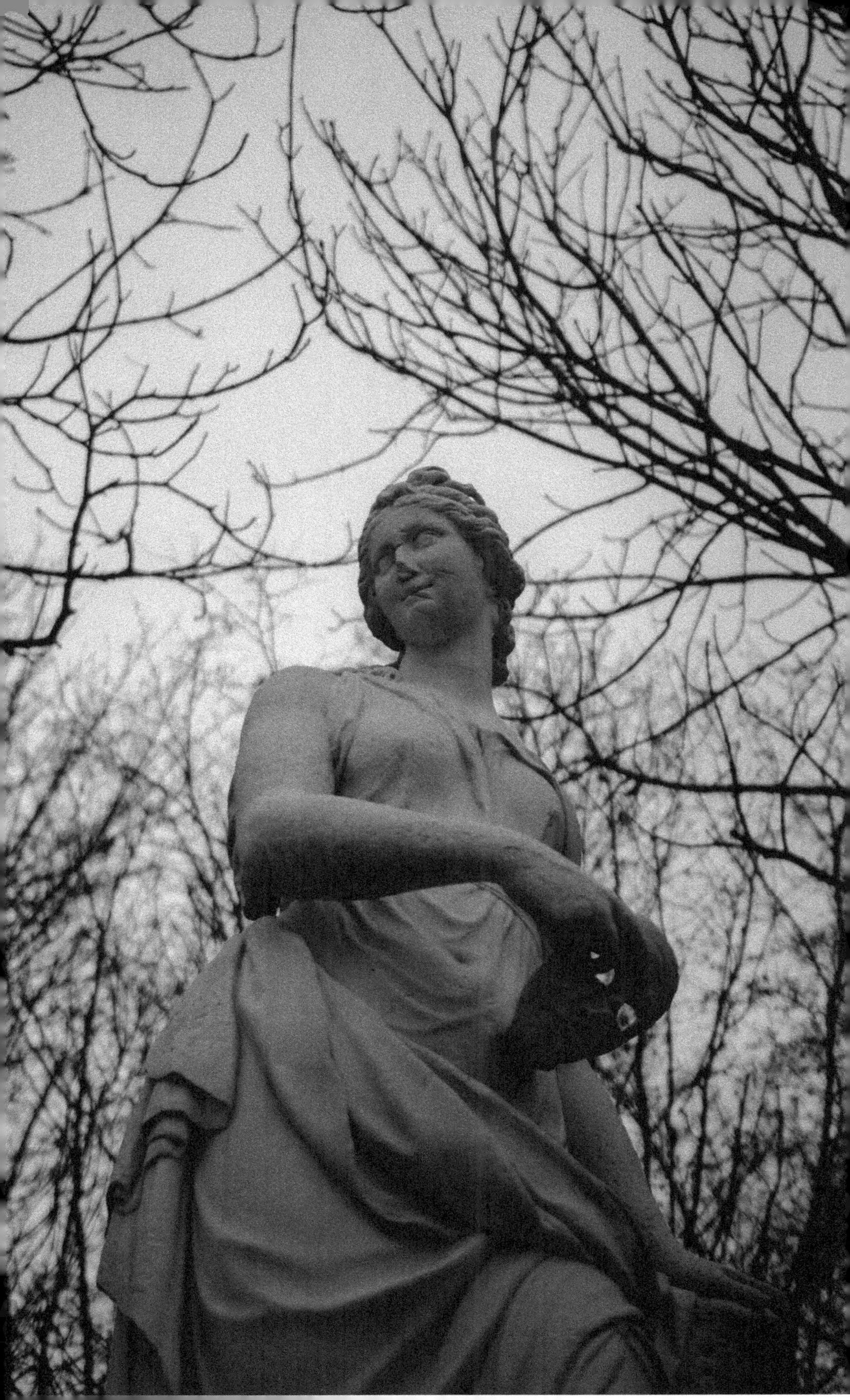

the mocking laugh of loneliness

the emptiness aches,
echoing in my soul,
reverberating sound but
bouncing off nothing.

it churns in my soul and waits.
claiming my attention at the worst moments.
reminding me my happiness,
is not real.

it hurts.
it pains.
day after day it chants my name,
it has nothing to do but remind me i'm not ok.

it owns my thoughts.
dulls my joy.
doubts my truth.
maniacally laughs when i collapse in fear.

i try to fill the space i lack.
praying and hoping to be saved,
but how can i be saved from something only i feel?
i wish i knew; i just want to heal.

a sucker born every minute

a lion in a cage paces,
competing in nonexistent races.

the ringmaster pokes and prods, never letting the aching lion sleep.
for the ringmaster knows he controls the lion's thoughts so he keeps him weak.

the lion's thoughts never rest.
drowning in a pool of inescapable worries, the need to be the best.

the lion pleads for the ringmaster to go,
but he laughs back in his face muttering, "no. no. no."

"you must listen to every thought.
no pause, remain distraught.

stay up, worry more.
never a chance to restore.

put on a show,
cover the pain so the audience won't know"

but the lion is tired of his own existence.
begging and pleading to the ringmaster with persistence,

"please just add some variety.
let me escape this circus of anxiety."

to be alone one must become accustomed to

silence.

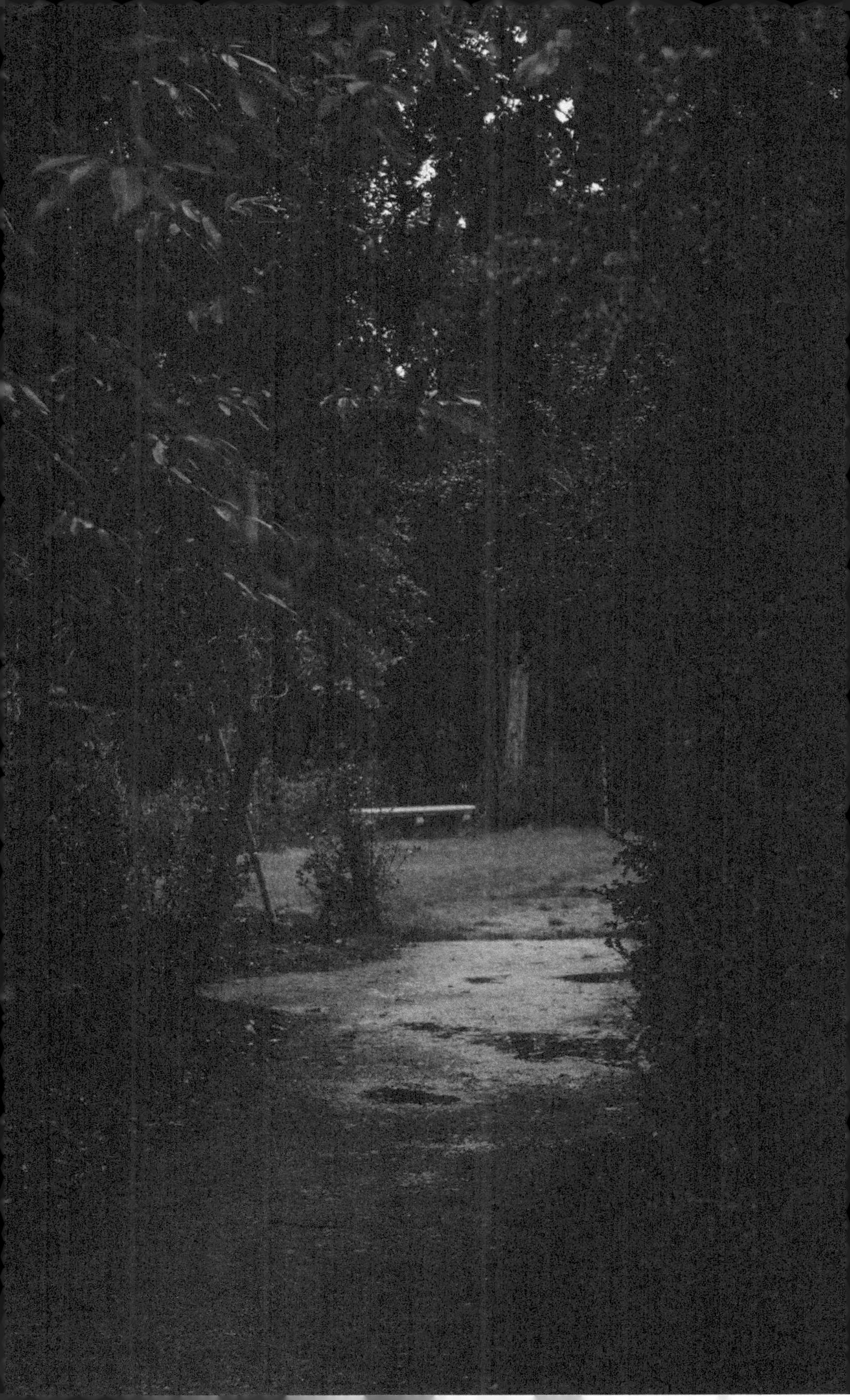

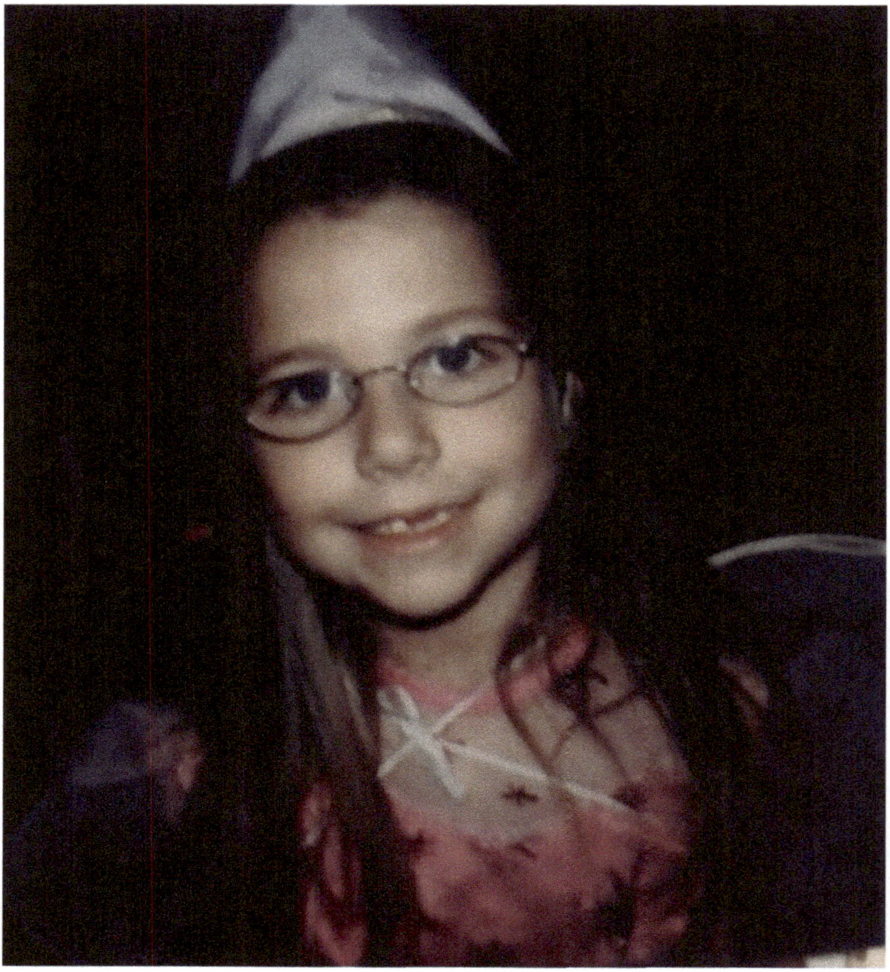

dream of my inner child

am standing. surrounded by darkness, cold and uncomfortable. i walk forward, ands outstretched. through the haze, i feel cold dark stone. i turn and feel another vall. all around me are walls. a maze. i scream. i cry. i plead for someone to hear me.
elp me.
run.
s fast as i can run. i can see nothing. i run into wall after wall. everywhere i turn i m trapped. i find a break. i squeeze through, barely fitting. though i am running i m gaining no ground, i am making no distance. seeing only haze, hitting only walls f the maze.
head there is a light, a small girl dressed in pink.
scream for her to run,
ut instead, she laughs.
am angry with her for being so foolish. for not listening to me. she is naive, unware of the darkness. i am irate at her innocence. i plead with her to run away, but nstead, she smiles at me with crooked teeth.
run towards her.
trip.
fall.
he darkness overwhelms me.
curl into a ball as words are hurled at my skin, stinging like needles.
you're not enough. you'll never be enough."
too big."
too small."
too ugly."
too tall."
unworthy. disgusting. embarrassing. hopeless. alone."
cry out in pain and cover my face.
hen she is there.
he looks down at me with pleading blue eyes,
get up, please get up. i need you to get up."
rise, aching, sore from the words. she grabs my hand and leads me. dragging her mall hand along the stone. to a clearing. the center of the maze. i follow her to a nirror encased in stone. i walk towards the glass, afraid, ashamed, insecure.
he stops.
he little girl looks at me through the reflection, "why did you convince me i wasn't nough?" she gently hands me a string and is gone, through the mirror. absorbed nto my reflection. i am left alone with only the maze.
or i am the master of the maze. trapped by the walls i have built. ever searching for he end of the string, lost in the labyrinth of my own creation. but led by the nwavering hope of the child within me.

clutches

like hands around my neck,
choking away my breath,
no inhale, no exhale.
my heart is pounding in my ears.
it is the only sound i can hear.
my chest hurts,
it burns.
i cover my head and try to calm myself.
i can't breathe.
my eyes ache, squeezing back tears.
i close them.
try to quiet the noise,
but it lives within me.
my own thoughts.
my own pain.
my own inability to cope.
i just want to be free,
but it's my own anxiety attacking me.

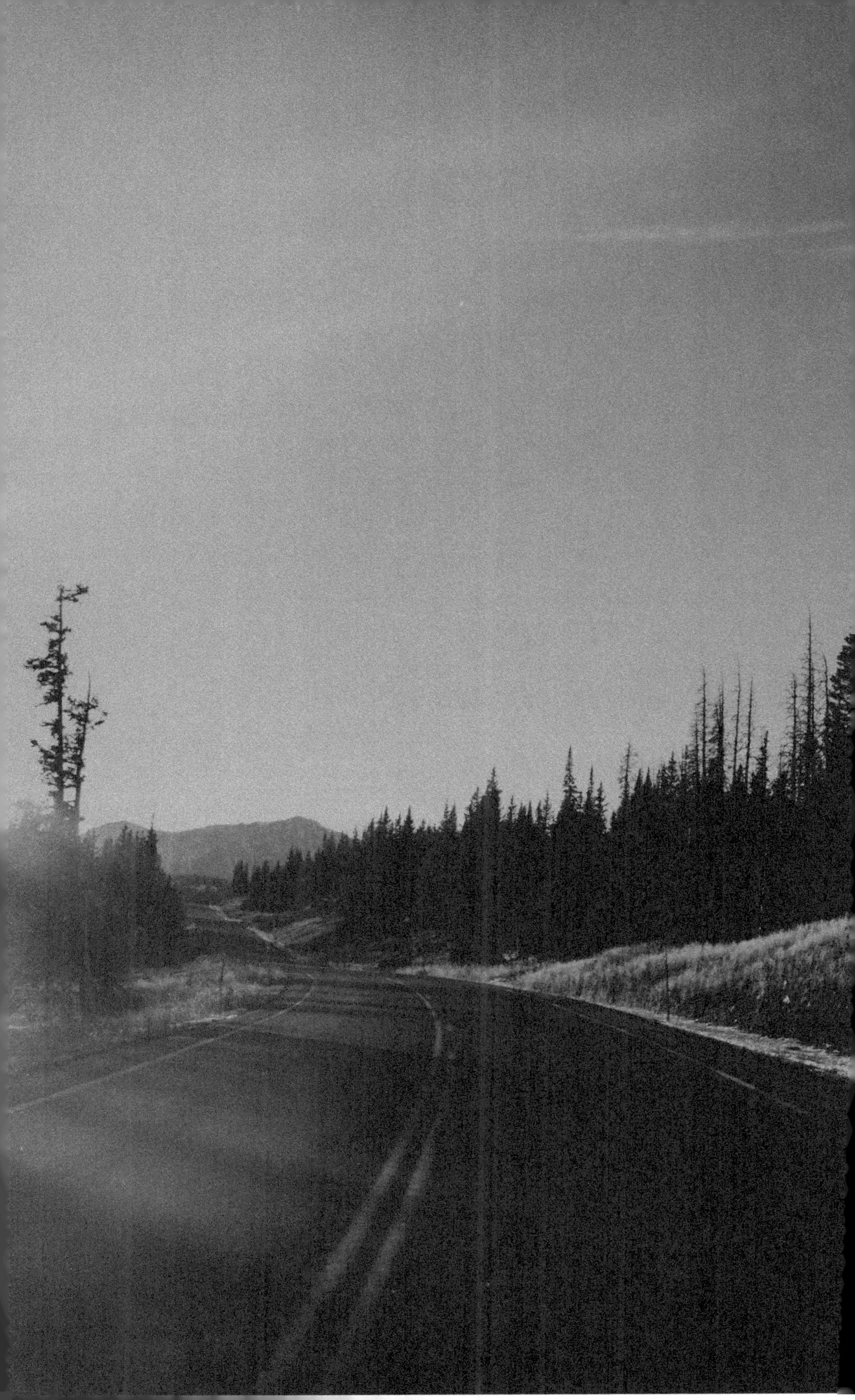

ballad of an enneagram type 3

i am not ok.
not "not ok" in the way of sadness or anger, but in the form of exhaustion.
i am weary.
i am so tired of fighting within myself;
the battle of who i am and who i want to be constantly grabbing me by the throat and choking the light out of me.
i constantly nod yes, saying "i'm alright" while i know in truth i am broken inside.
but broken in a way only i can fix.

i am exhausted from constantly pushing and working myself.
exhausted from never being able to relax.
exhausted from pushing towards things at such speed i leave myself in the dirt.
exhausted with never being able to show myself even the slightest bit of patience.
exhausted with my inner monologue stealing away moments that are supposed to be filled with joy.
exhausted from being wound so tightly if i'm not working and striving towards my goals,
i am consumed with the need to do so.
exhausted from thinking i'm never enough.
even in moments i am supposed to be filled with hope, the anxiety of not buildimg something that places me closer to the end goal steals my precious moments.

but what is the end goal?
when i have accomplished everything i told myself i needed to, will i finally be able to be happy?
or will i look at myself, filled with the illusion of success, only to find myself still broken?
i want to be able to exist in both worlds, to be content and fufill my purpose.
i see it breathe effortlessly all around me, but it is stifled within me.
will it always be this way?
will i remain trapped in myself?

or will i learn to let people help me;
to stop expecting myself to carry the weight of the world alone?
will i give myself the patience i deserve?
will i see that maybe, just maybe, i've done enough?
recognize that sometimes all i have to do is the next best thing,
and know that it is possible for someone to love me for exactly who i am,
to love my bare and broken soul in such a way that i stop striving.

so, i learn.
i set different goals for myself.
to be patient even when the voice within me is screaming that i'm not enough,
to be kind to myself even when i want to tear myself apart,
to let people in,
to show weakness,
to be ok with vulnerability and learn to trust.
to show up as i am.
to be brave when i am timid.
to risk.
to hurt.
to heal.
to choose living over chasing a perfect life.

i work to change my mindset.
it a slow and painful process,
but day by day i grow.
i learn to act from compassion not competition.
i learn that missing a day doesn't make me a failure.
i learn that i am my own worst critic.
i learn that who i am is not wrapped in what i do or do not accomplish.
i learn that i am worthy of love.
and slowly, and oh so gently,
i wake up.
i seize every day.
and i realize that i may not be now, but someday,
i will be ok.

get comfortable with failure and accustomed to discomfort.
failure proves you tried and discomfort produces growth.

the butterfly doesn't know it is beautiful; it just spreads its wings.

could it be us?

if given the chance,
i would love your pain away.
i would wade through the darkness to find the center of you,
the one pulsing point that is true.
the part that you thought had taken all the pain it could,
laid down and died.
the broken, twisted, blacked part of yourself you
desperately try to hide.
i'd bear your shame with a smile on my face.
hoping, dreaming, praying that your wounds would rest
comfortably in my safe space.
that every word you couldn't bring yourself to say,
every thought, hope, scar, all of you would nestle in and choose to stay.
i can carry the weight of you,
in fact it would be an honor to.
i see you as you are, scared, hurt, deeming yourself
unworthy of love,
and i stand in front of you offering all that i am made of.
yet, the light at the center of my darkness whispers,

"what do they see?"

"could they witness my darkness and still love me?"

"could they handle the depth of whomever i may be?'

"could i finally be free?"

if i bore my heart, faced my fear, and loved you,

do you think you could love me too?

perhaps there is no greater risk in life than letting ourselves be loved.

careful casting

i have spent years of my life bringing myself to nothing, attempting to ignite the flames of others. then the right people stepped into my life. they placed their hands around my flame and protected me from letting myself give myself away. they tended to the smouldering ember inside of me and willed me back to a burn. they scooped the wax i had become for you and molded me. i was malleable in the heat of their hands, but they chose to reshape me into an image of myself. they didn't need to be lit; they burned bright enough to help me reignite myself. they were so conscious of me they monitored my flame, attempting to break me from giving it away. and unknown to them they showed me what love feels like. i'm now able to see the people who want to melt me, take me, and make me a part of themselves: dry brittle wicks, desperate to consume the flame of others, people who don't produce their own heat and steal the spark of another. for the first time, because of the love of others, i see it and i turn away. i don't destroy myself to be the thing they need me to be. i am a candle, safe in their hands, they don't blow me out, they just let me burn. and beckon me, brighter, brighter...

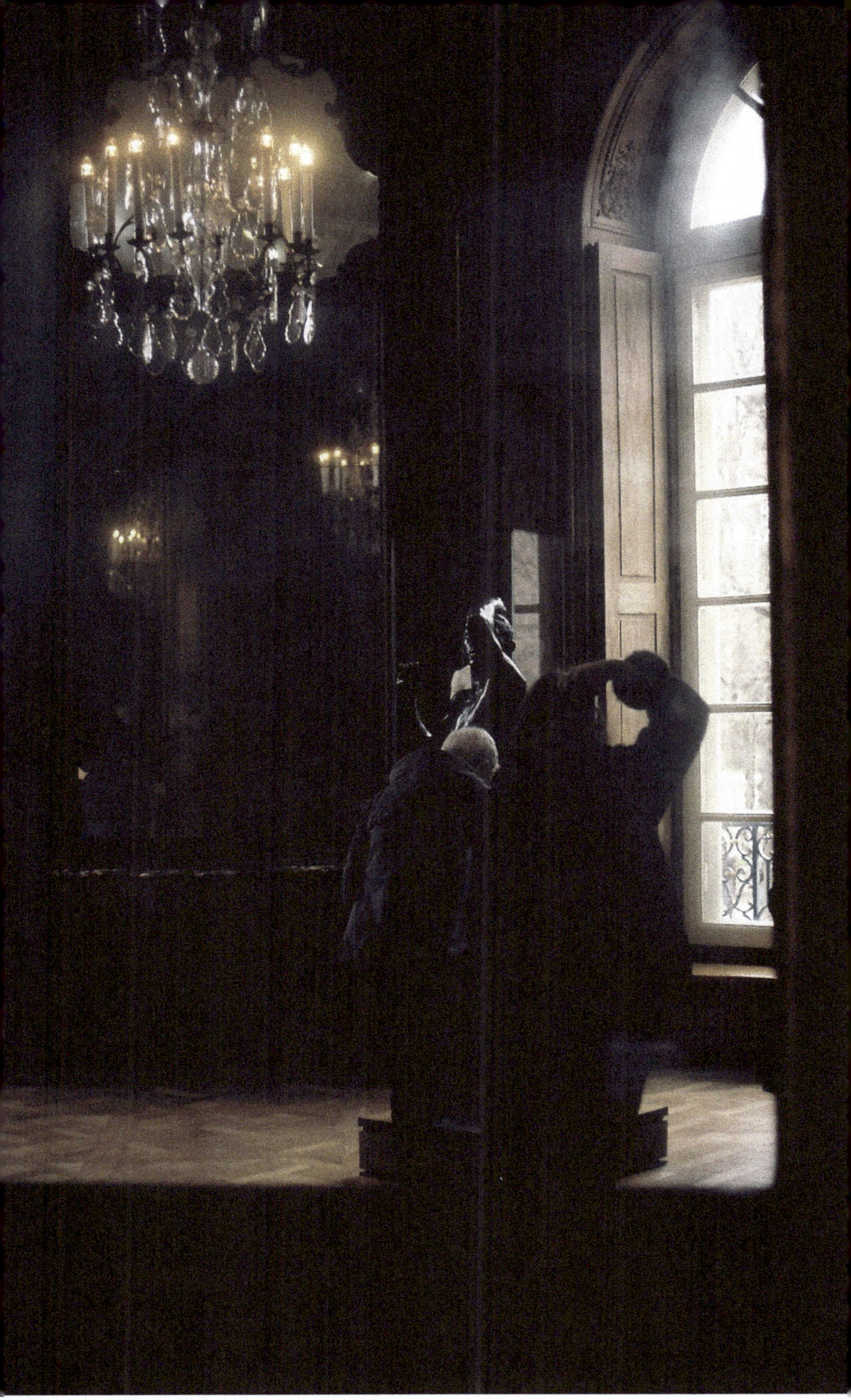

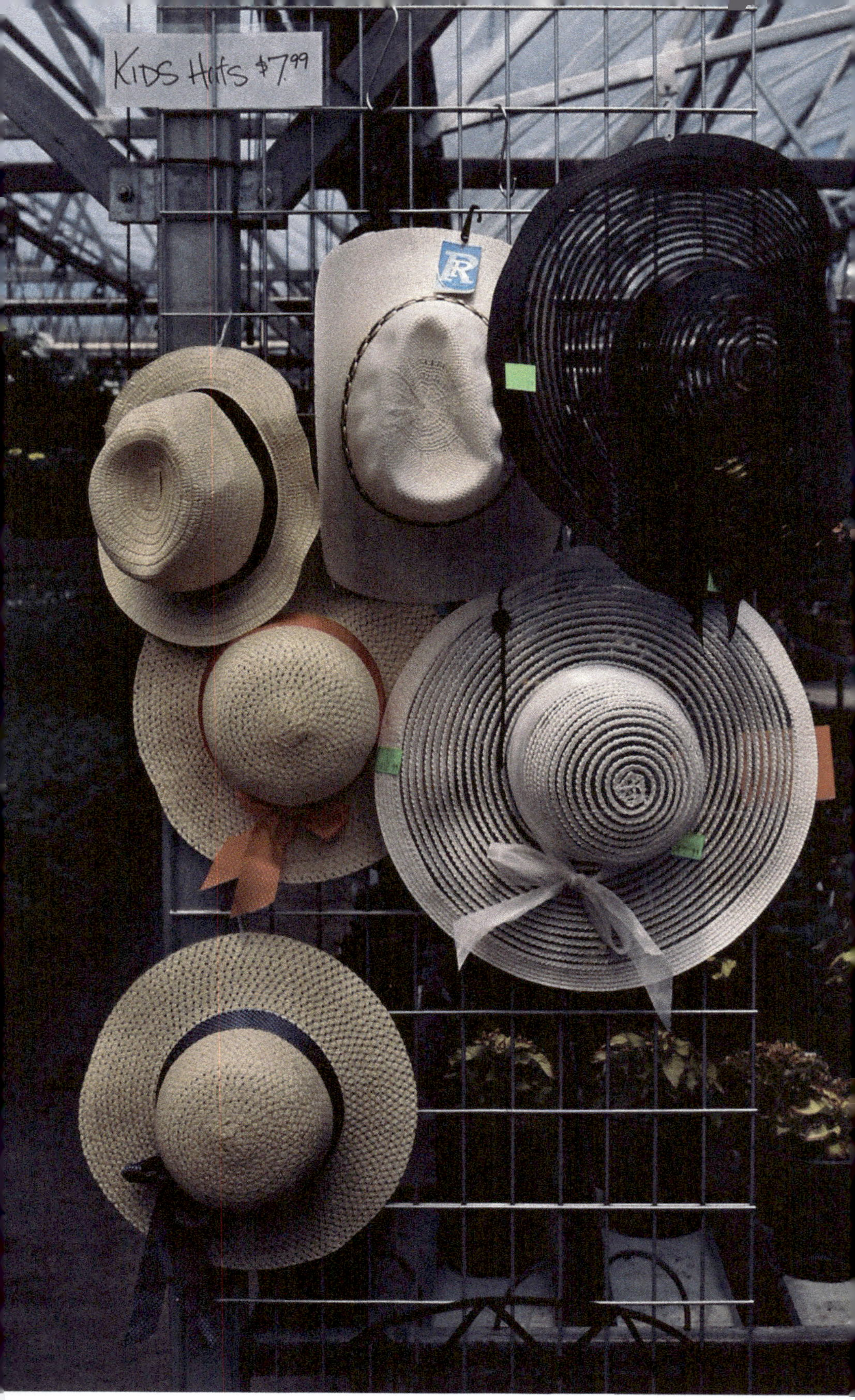
KIDS Hats $7.99

THE FIRST PAGE OF A NEW NOTEBOOK
THE MORNING AFTER A WINTER SNOWSTORM
A BLANK CANVAS
SUMMER LIGHT POURING THROUGH OPEN WINDOWS
WATCHING STORM CLOUDS ROLL
YOU AND ME NESTLED TOGETHER
FLOWER GARDENS
ALL THINGS BEST FELT AND OBSERVED
ENCASED IN THE SERENITY OF
SILENCE.

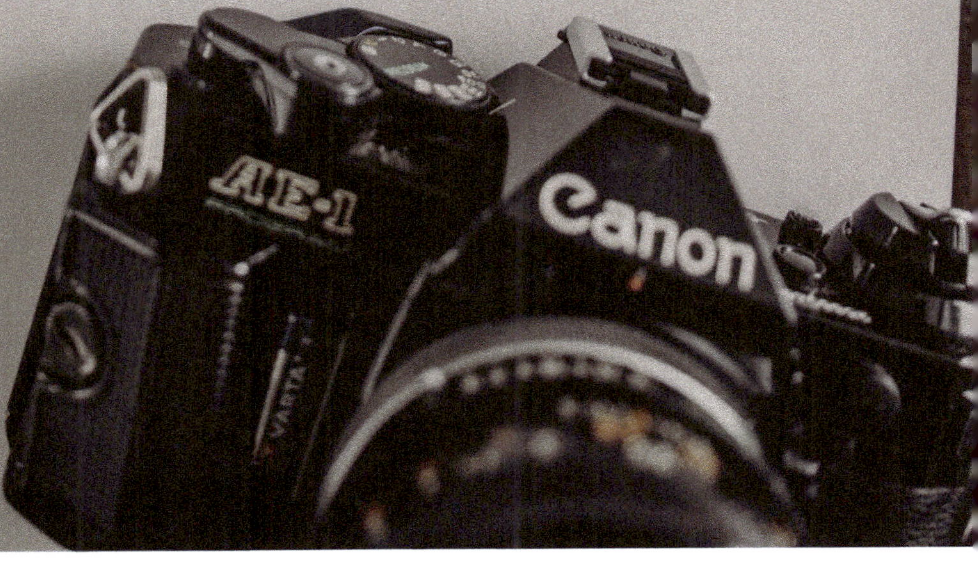

there was during you

to be truly loved is a complex thing because in me i find a raw, broken, and bleeding person, desperately trying to feel whole. but i can no longer pretend. i have to be. i cannot fake a smile and mask the confusion in my soul. he sees straight through me. when i am forced to lay down all of the weapons i hold in defense of my own insecurity, i realize that i was so busy building walls i forgot to plant the garden. i was so busy lying to myself and trying to maintain an image of perfection, i forgot to be me. so here i am, in ruins, standing in front of a boy trying to be something i've never had to be, real. but i don't know how. in this journey of finding love, i realized the hardest thing to do was to find myself. like salt being poured on a slug, the image i thought i was holding withered away and all that is left is me. scared to take the baby steps once so easy because i don't know me. i don't know who i am meant to be. maybe he can help tell me. in the meantime, i'll trade my rose-colored glasses for his because maybe if i could see myself through his eyes, i'd know where to begin.

then there was after you

i used to sit patiently, waiting for you to tell me who you wanted me to be, and calling it love. i shifted and changed myself to fit your mold, breaking myself into pieces you would be able to hold. i lied to myself and believed that if i was able to see myself through your eyes, i might truly see me. that if i planted enough of the flowers you liked in the garden of myself, you would want to stay. you would like the image enough to finally stop asking me to change. you would stop taking out your own insecurities on me and i would not have to tiptoe around your perception of who you thought i should be. the spirit inside of me begged to return but i kept her at bay afraid of your rejection. i wanted you to love me so i could feel worthy of love. i twisted my truth, convinced myself i loved you, but deep inside of myself i alway knew. but then on a tuesday in november, sitting on my bedroom floor, six months after you, i realized that harsh love brings to light a painful question:

how can i truly love someone and be loved truly, without first loving myself?

if i don't first find myself how could i expect someone else to find me? it's an impossible task to ask of someone else. others do not know my pain. my light. what keeps me up at night. i can see through my heart, break it apart, put it back together, and heal myself. no one can love me like i can. no one knows what flowers i want to plant in the garden of my heart. but i do. i built the walls around the garden. protected it. planted daily. tended to her. breathed life into the petals on the ground. watered the wilting flowers. pulled the weeds planted by the world. tending to that which i love. love doesn't scale the walls, force itself into my eden. real love stands at the gate. hopeful but patient. love waits. love honors. love does not push, prod, shape, or change me to fit their reality. love carries a shovel and plants with me. love tenderly holds my flowers in their hands. admiring every petal and adoring unconditionally. and the answer to my pain is a simple fact: love is not love if it comes with a list of demands. love should fall in step alongside the path of you, strolling in comfortable solitude, holding hands.

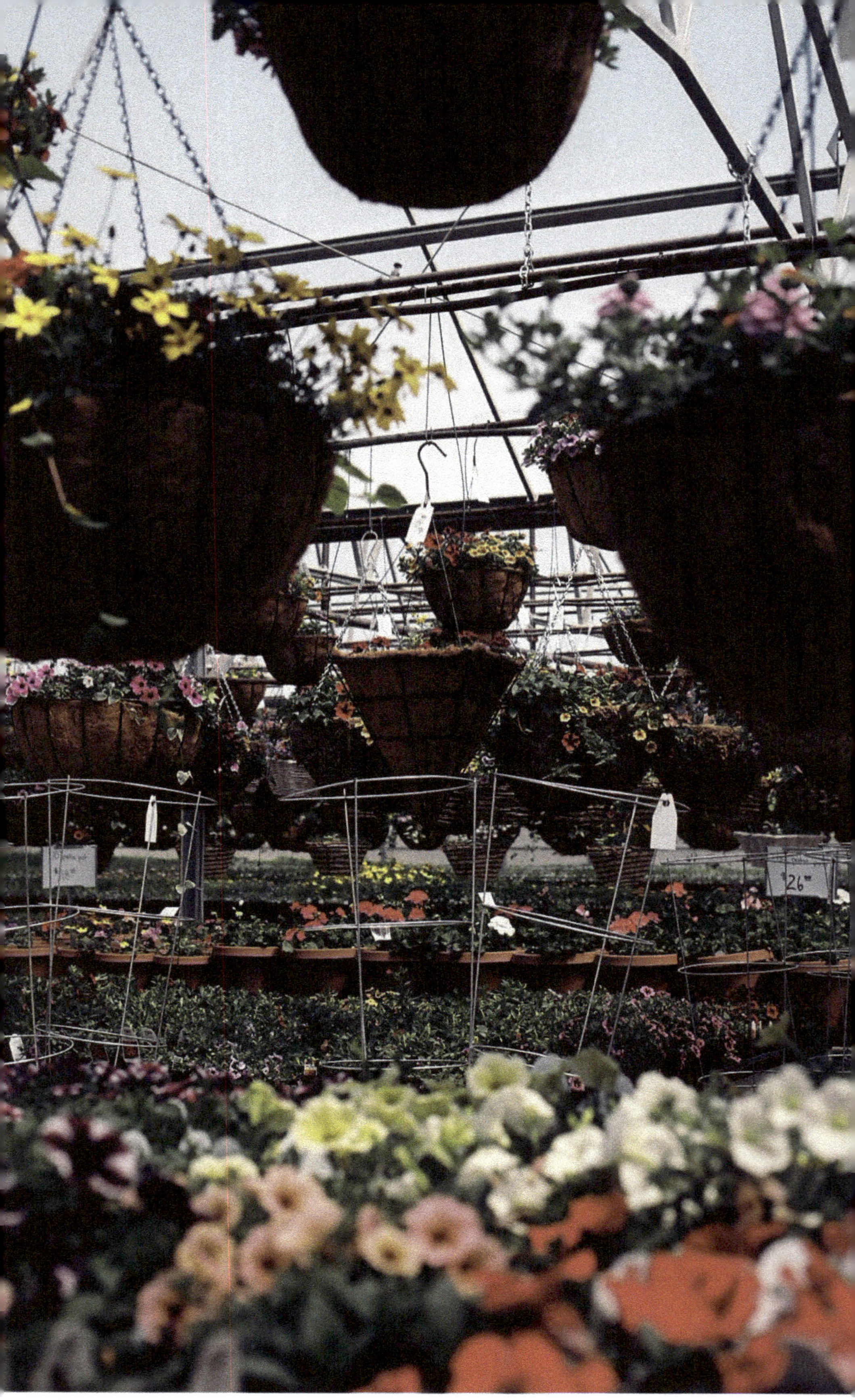
26

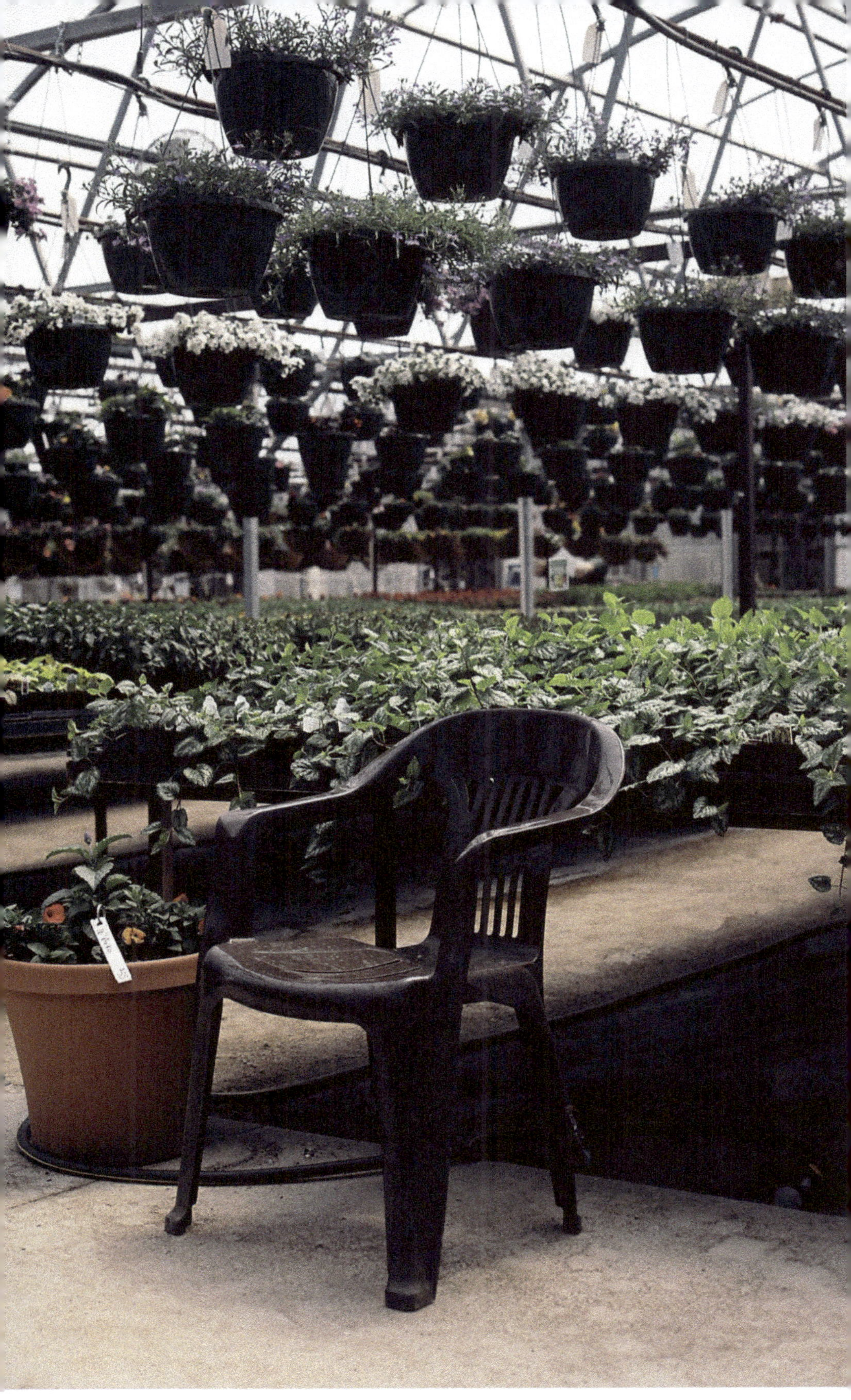

if we desire to be admired, adored, or lusted after, what feeble confidence that produces. for finding worth in the gaze of others is a rapidly evaporating reality.

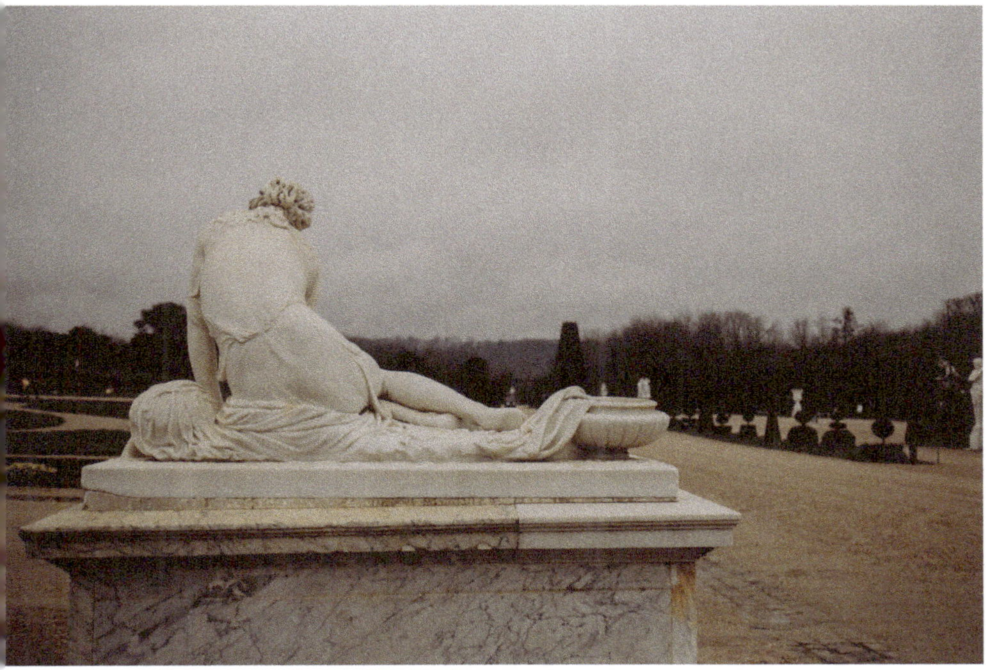

her

one day she woke up and chose herself.
she conquered the opinions of the insignificant.
abandoned the doubts she had clung to for a reason
unknown to herself,
and chose her soul.
finally, she was free and what a sight she was to see,
a woman unafraid to stare into the face of destiny.

she

who am i to think i can be great?
to think i have something to give?
the influence to change tides and lessen blows?
to wake daily, thinking i can become someone?
who am i to pride myself so highly?

yet, who am i not to?
who am i to lessen me?
to tighten the reins of possibility.
why do i cower,
why do i fear?

who am i to deem me unworthy?
who am i to say no?
who am i to say i can't dream?
to quiet the voice in my soul,
screaming to stand.
to show them
to take the blows
to be unwavering
to dare to doubt me.

who am i to not be?
i am she.

unbreakable poise

my whole life i had been taught to believe that i was the only gazelle among a pride of lions.
vulnerable, afraid, silent.
always watching my back, expecting the next attack.
until i realized, in fact, i am the lion among gazelles.
or more correctly, and more deadly, the lioness.
in control.
in charge.
always hunting.
no longer the prey but the predator.
the inverse of a reality rarely seen but blatantly true.
for it is i who intimidates the gazelle,
the one who makes them recoil and question.
the one who stares into the eyes of lions, unflinching.
a lioness unprotected yet respected.
my presence always felt.
refusing to accept the hand i've been dealt.
making the gazelle's weak hearts fear change.
for they know a beast like me is strange.
me a so-called freak makes their souls bleak.
for at a sway of my hips and a word from my lips,
their countenance flips,
and i am in control.
my uniqueness gives me power.
although i appear a delicate flower,
i am the storm that breaks the trees,
makes kings fall to their knees.
i stand out from the rest,
for in this position, i am my best,
no longer a gazelle but instead a lioness.

the view from up here

you ask me what i fear
in truth, there is not much to hear.

i quake at the thought of simply wasting my life,
falling victim to the woes of every struggle and strife.

not making a difference, not giving it my best,
and instead settling to be complacent like the rest.

insecure and doubting my own worth,
consumed with the opinions of everyone on earth.

hoping only to reach the next milestone,
never looking up from my phone.

i don't want my days to wither away,
i want to make the most of little things, like flowers in may.

feeling sunshine on my face,
holding the keys to my first place.

cooking in the kitchen on rainy days,
the way the world slows when don williams plays.

for the only promise kept is the end,
and it is not our friend.

when i reach the end, i want to take a bow, knowing i had done all that i could,
having enjoyed my life's tiny perfect moments as fearlessness should.

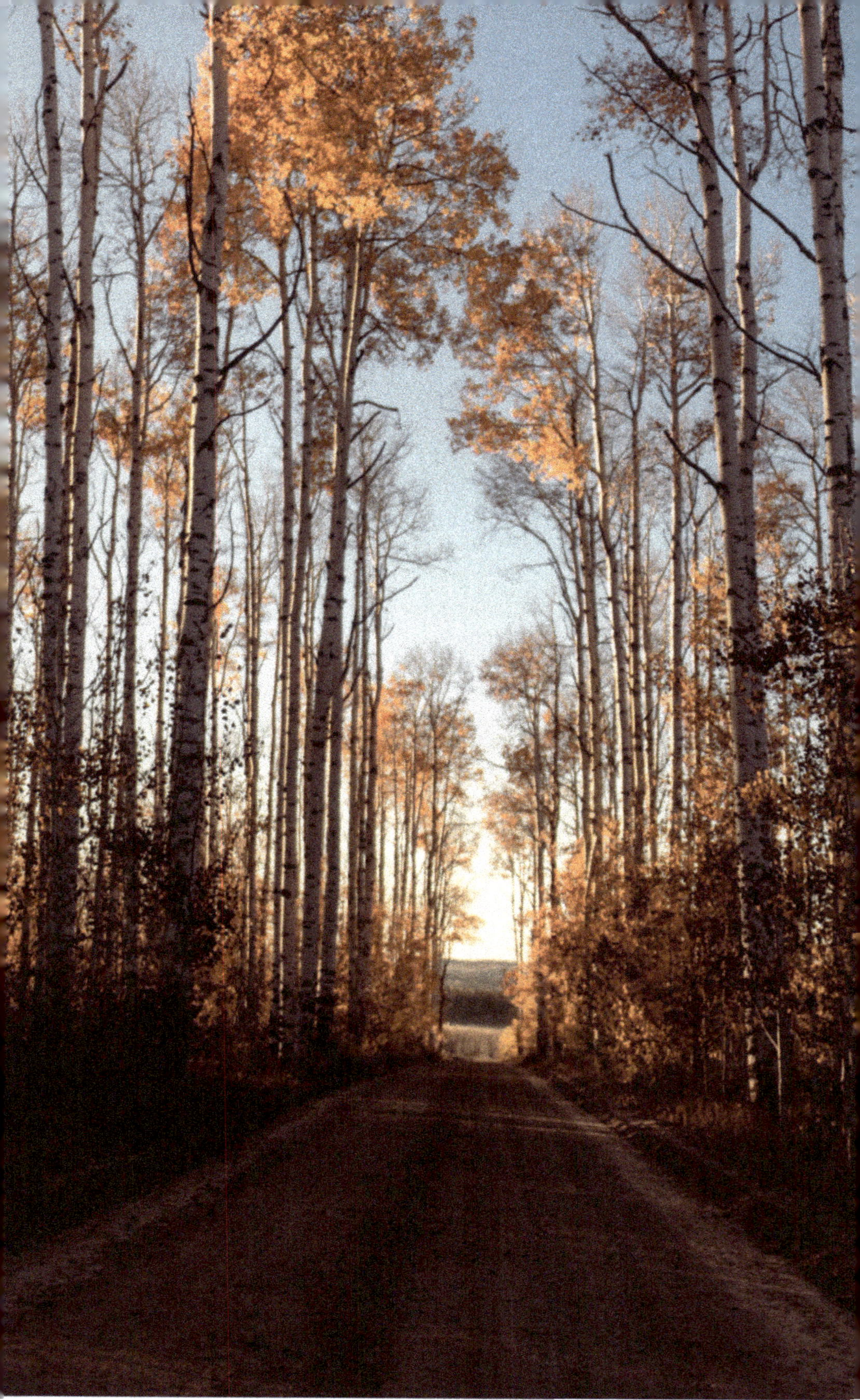

and so is the cycle of the leaves

a complex phenomenon exists within me. i have an intense nostalgia for things i have never experienced. i yearn for moments i have never lived but feel as though i have.

it occupies my thoughts as i am constantly dreaming of how things will be or how i hope they are. at times it makes me numb. my nostalgia makes things that are actually happening fall short of my expectations, plummeting me into disappointment, making my life appear worthless.

at times, it makes me love so deeply and with so much intensity, that it hurts. all of my sadness and joy swirling together until my emotions can only be released in tears. i am so overwhelmed by the love i feel for others that i cannot express to them how much they mean to me, how blessed i am by them, and how much i will someday miss them. it weighs over my shoulders like a quilt, comforting me but simultaneously dragging me down. i constantly grapple for the words to say but as quickly as i can grab them, they float away, like leaves in the wind. for i know, like leaves, the ones i love will not always be with me. i know some hear my words and others don't. i am left to only pray that they know at that moment they have seen my soul. hoping that they know that they are the nostalgia i long for.

it makes many moments bittersweet. my heart breaks at the fact i will only get to live in this perfection once. in moments when my world is everything i had dreamed and my hope is existing in front of me, i pause, and embrace, so full of life i feel as though i could burst. but i recognize that the exact moment i am living will never happen again. so, i pause, inhale deeply, and observe slowly, breathing in a memory. for i know, the pain and bliss i feel simultaneously is all that it can be, all that is within it, and all that will be. and it is called life.

run away & don't come back

the land is calling, and i must go.
searching for skies filled with sun and snow.
all i want is you and me.
in a place unknown, totally free.

step onto the road less traveled,
be done with pavement; find the gravel.
fill a backpack, let's be alone.
find a place where we're free to roam.
just say yes, grab my hand.
let's search for a world that isn't planned.

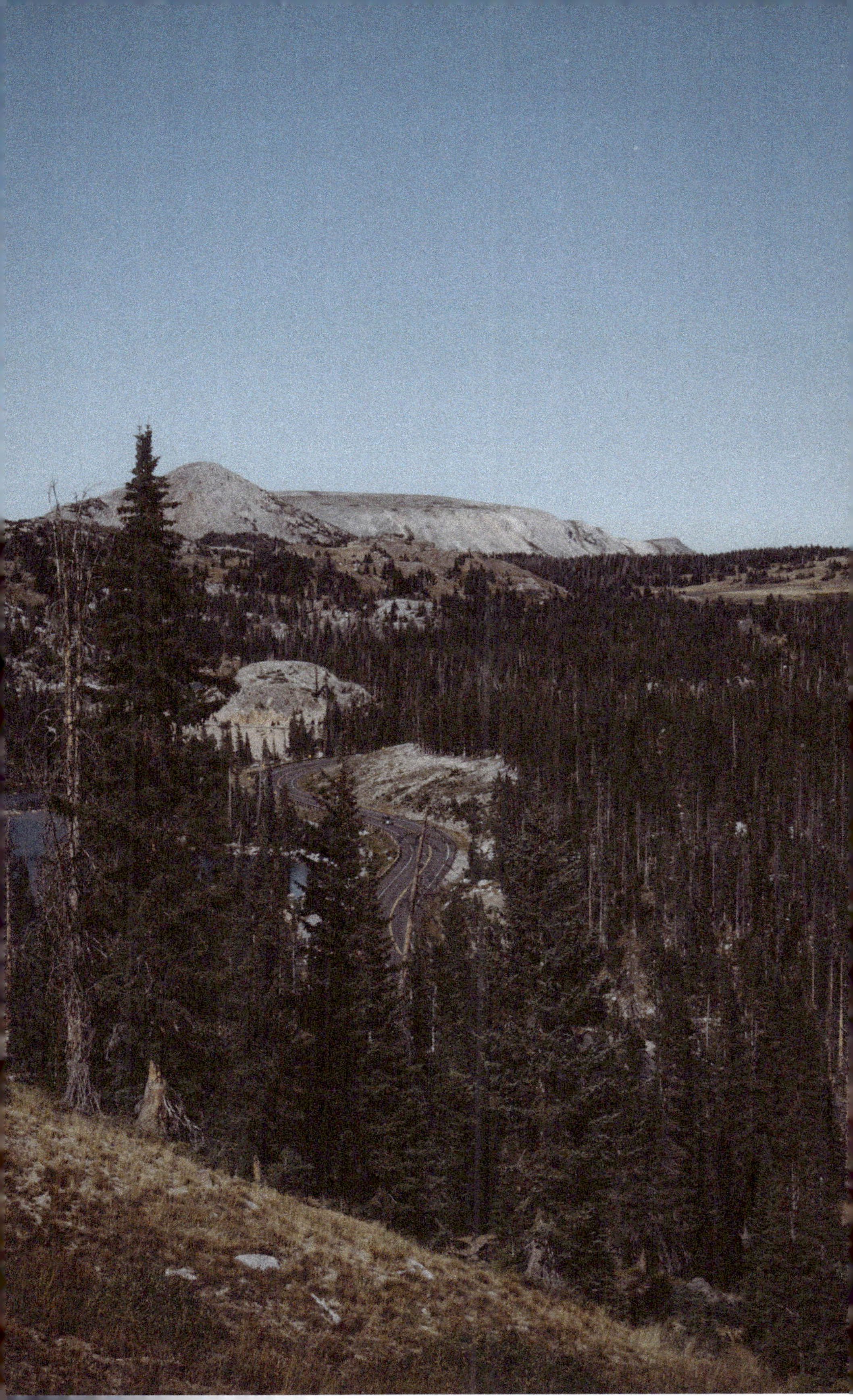

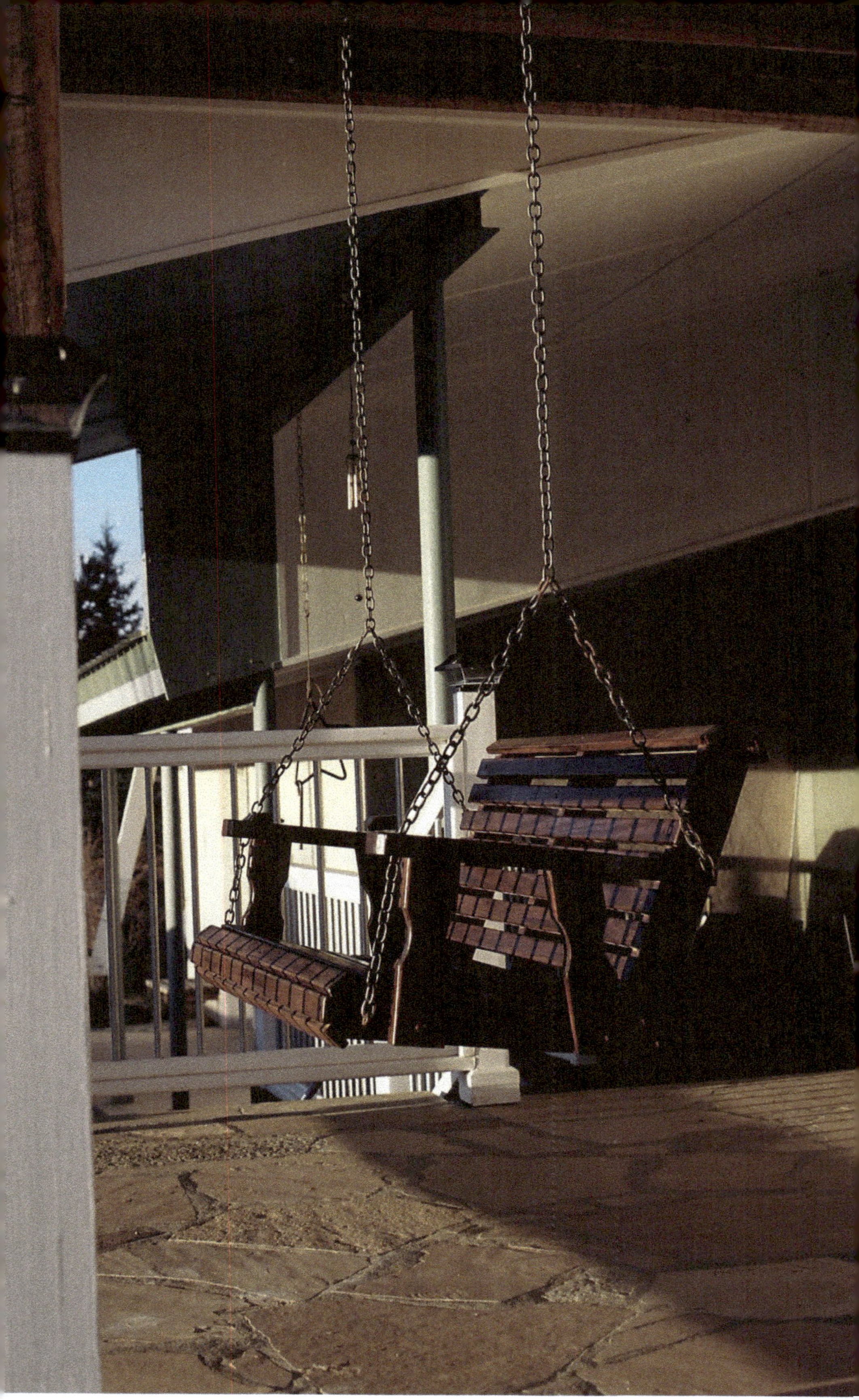

if there is a place or a person that quiets your soul and causes your worries to cease, be there. life is too short to waste in nonpeaceful places.

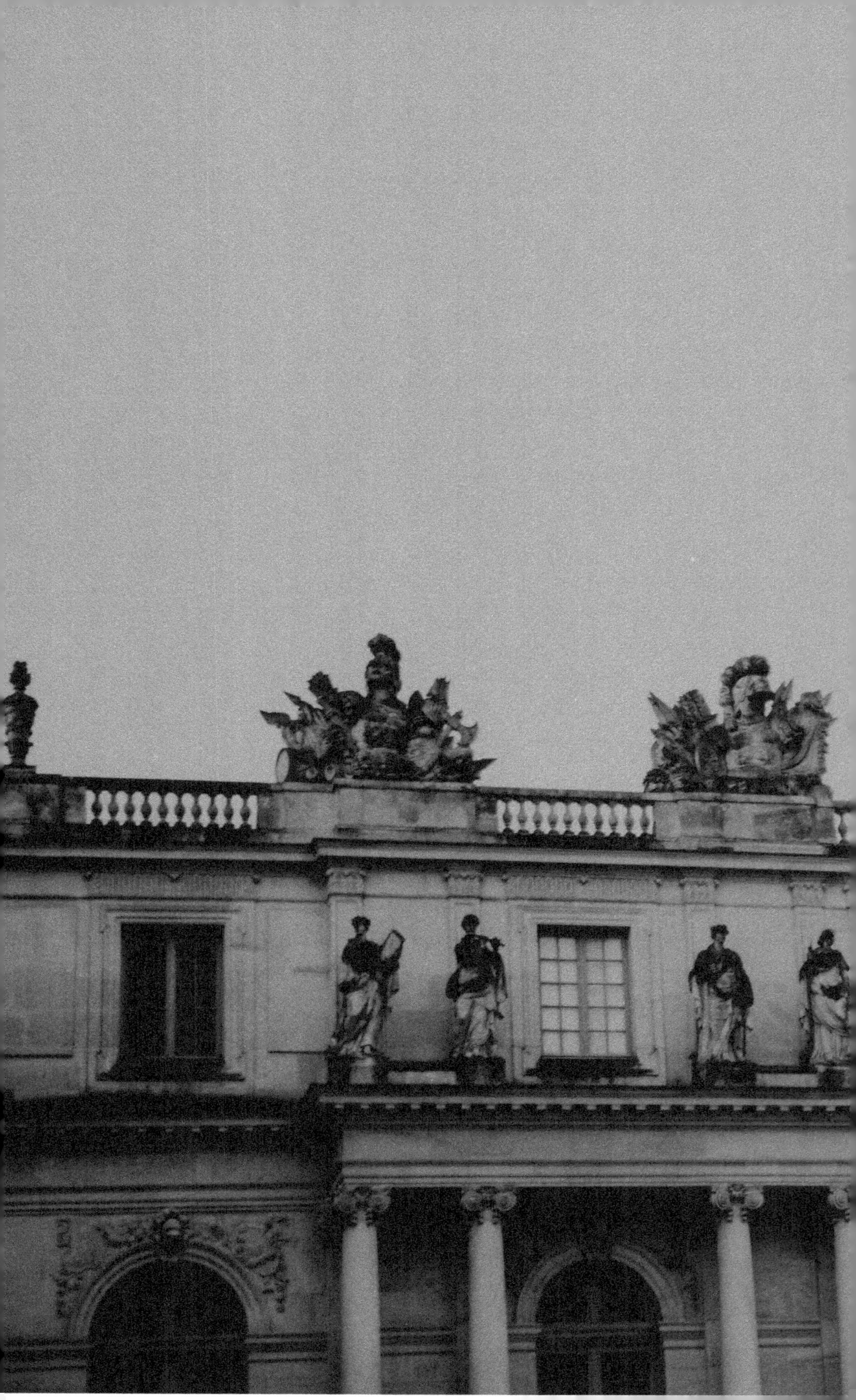

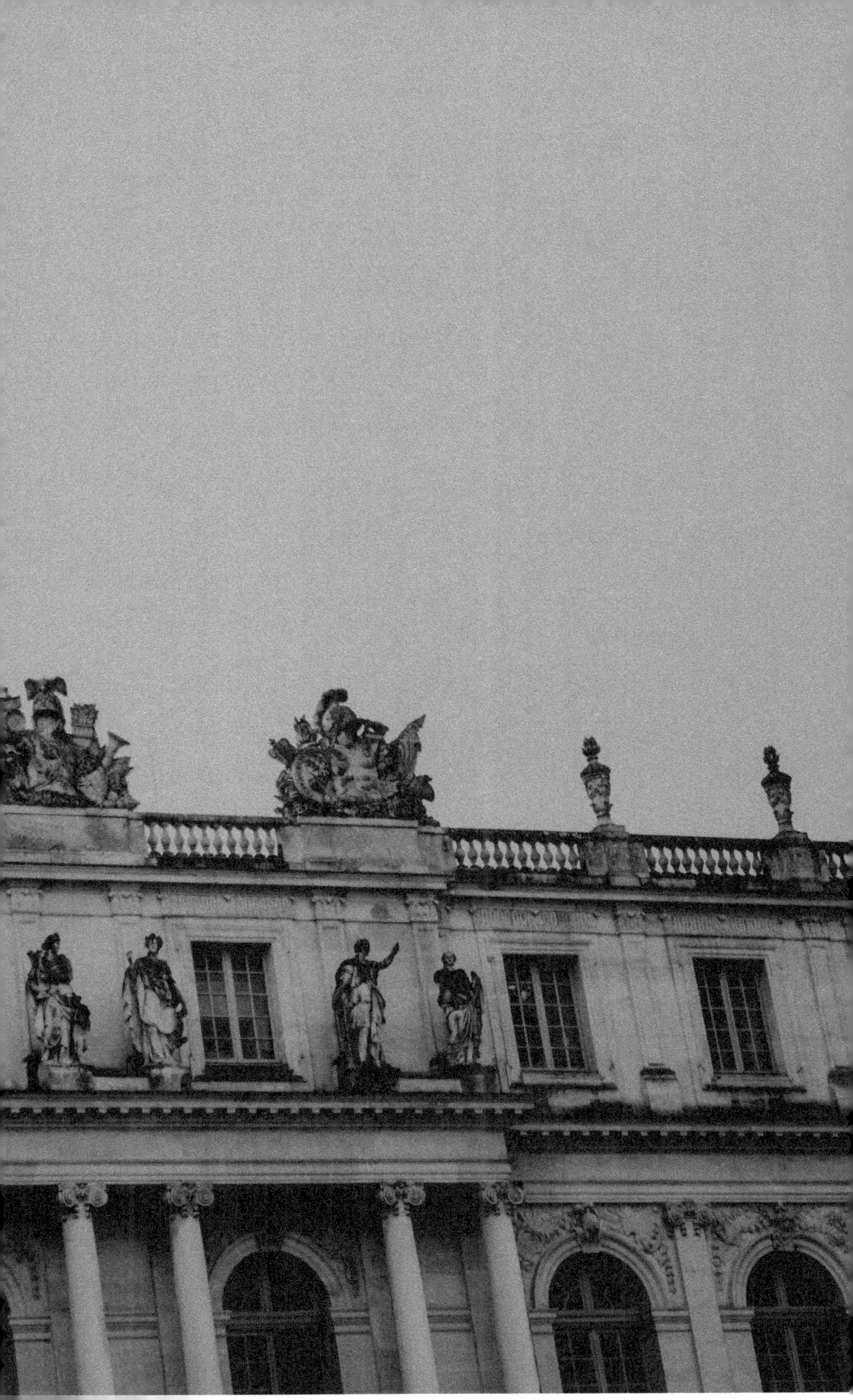

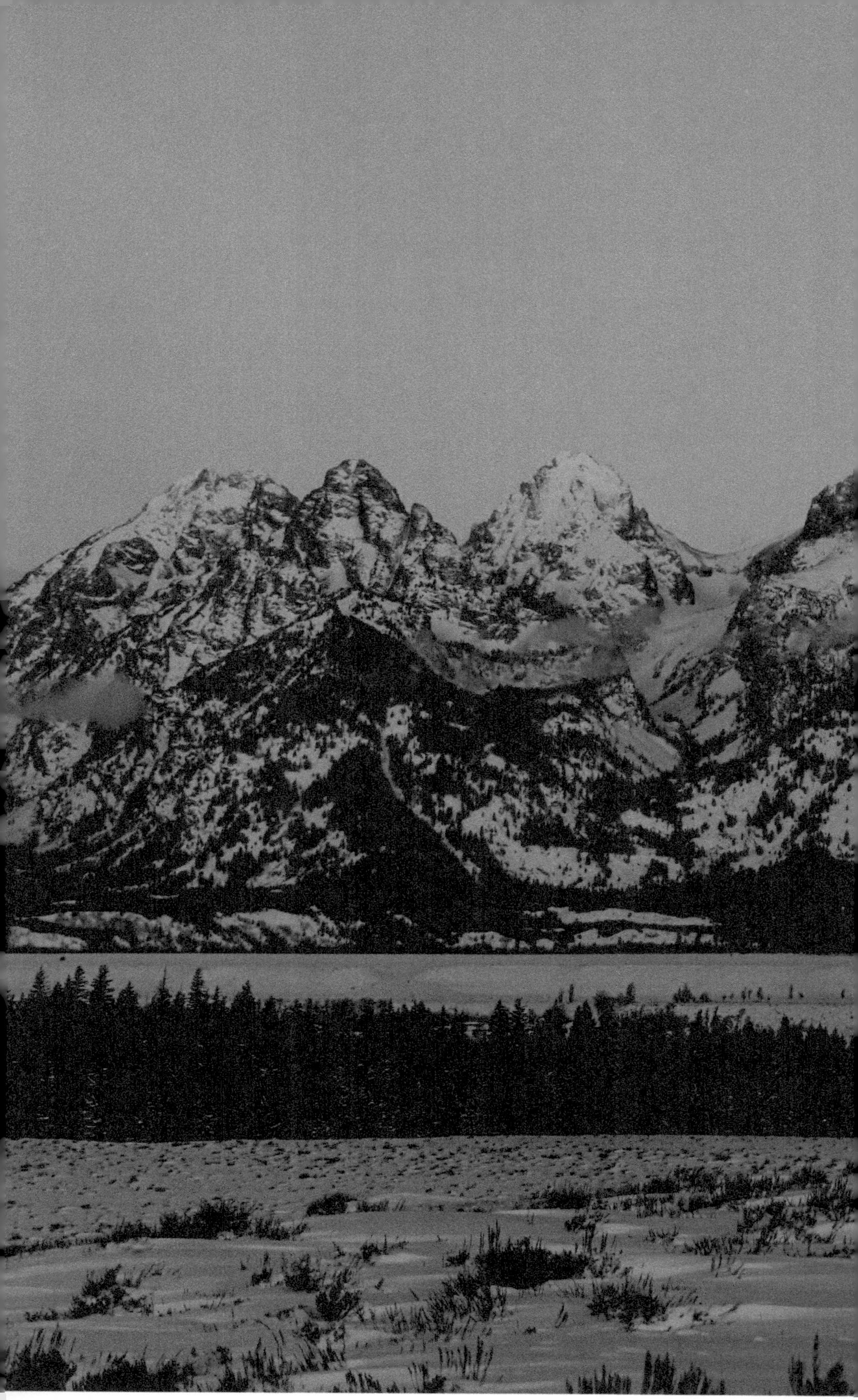

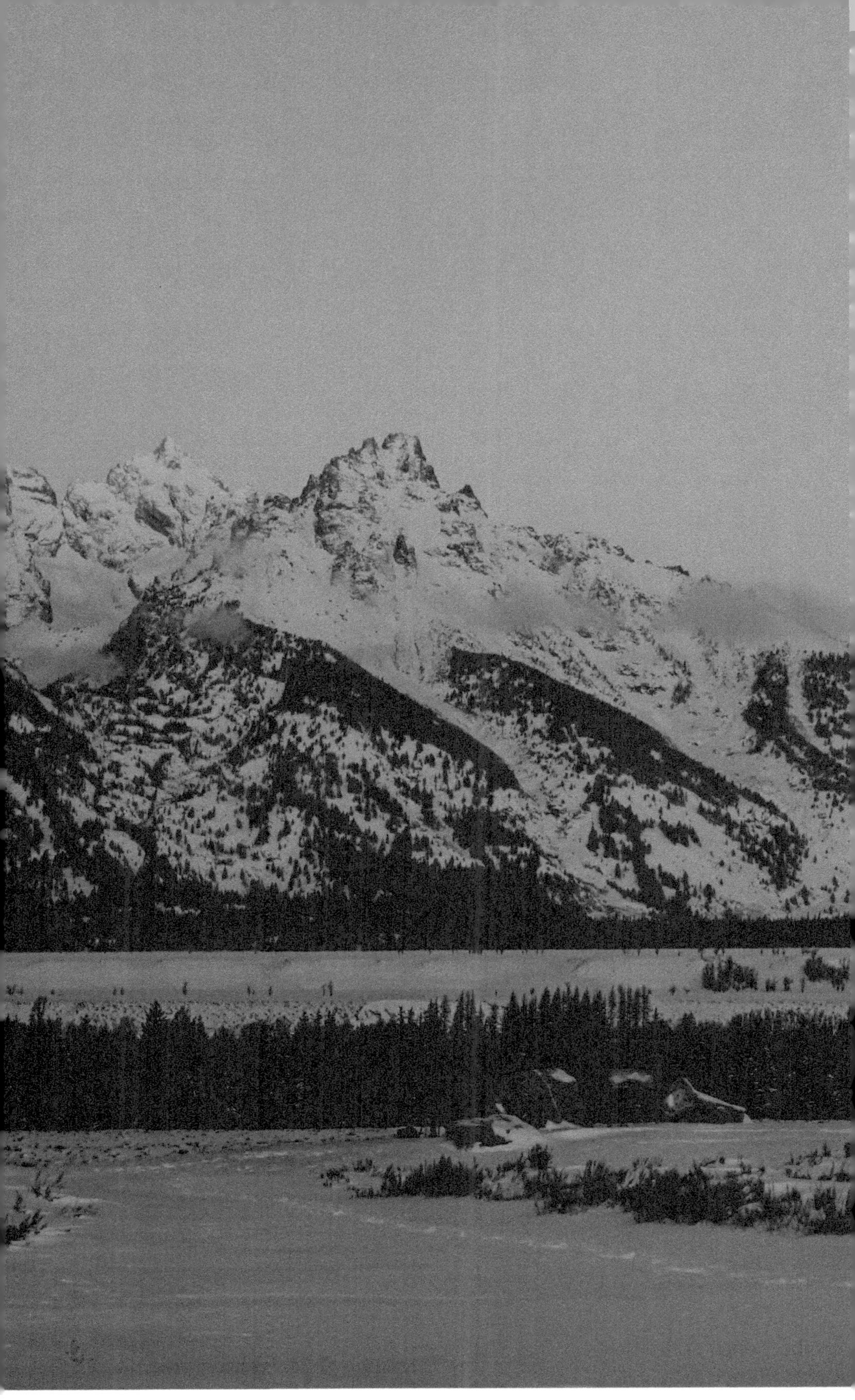

reverie

on the days when the world becomes too much to bear,
i drift into the simple serenity of a space created in my mind.
it is an early morning, a blissful morning.
the air smells faintly of the snowstorm rolling in,
the chill reddening my cheeks and awakening my soul.
the clouds are billowing and rolling over the mountains, content with their pace.
they do not race, and for once, neither do my thoughts.
i have turned on the gentle music that makes me feel whole,
and it plays softly while i pour my coffee, filled with cinnamon swirls and the lingering scent of nutmeg.
i put on my favorite pair of warm woolen socks and grab the quilt that rests along the back of my worn couch,
wrapping it around me, cloaking myself in its warmth.
with my coffee radiating a satisfying comfort into my palm,
i open the door.
to the most exquisite of masterpieces,
an oasis,
my soul space.
mountains, trees, a lake,
space, silence, and serenity.
cold air rushes into my lungs, chilling me,
the simplicity of an inhale reminding me of the beauty of being alive.
i rest.
comfortable on my porch lulled by the rocking of my chair,
i am warm.
i am safe.
content in my space.
spending my morning in my happy place,
a sanctuary of my own creation,
the hope of a place that finally feels like home,
a dream nestled in my imagination.

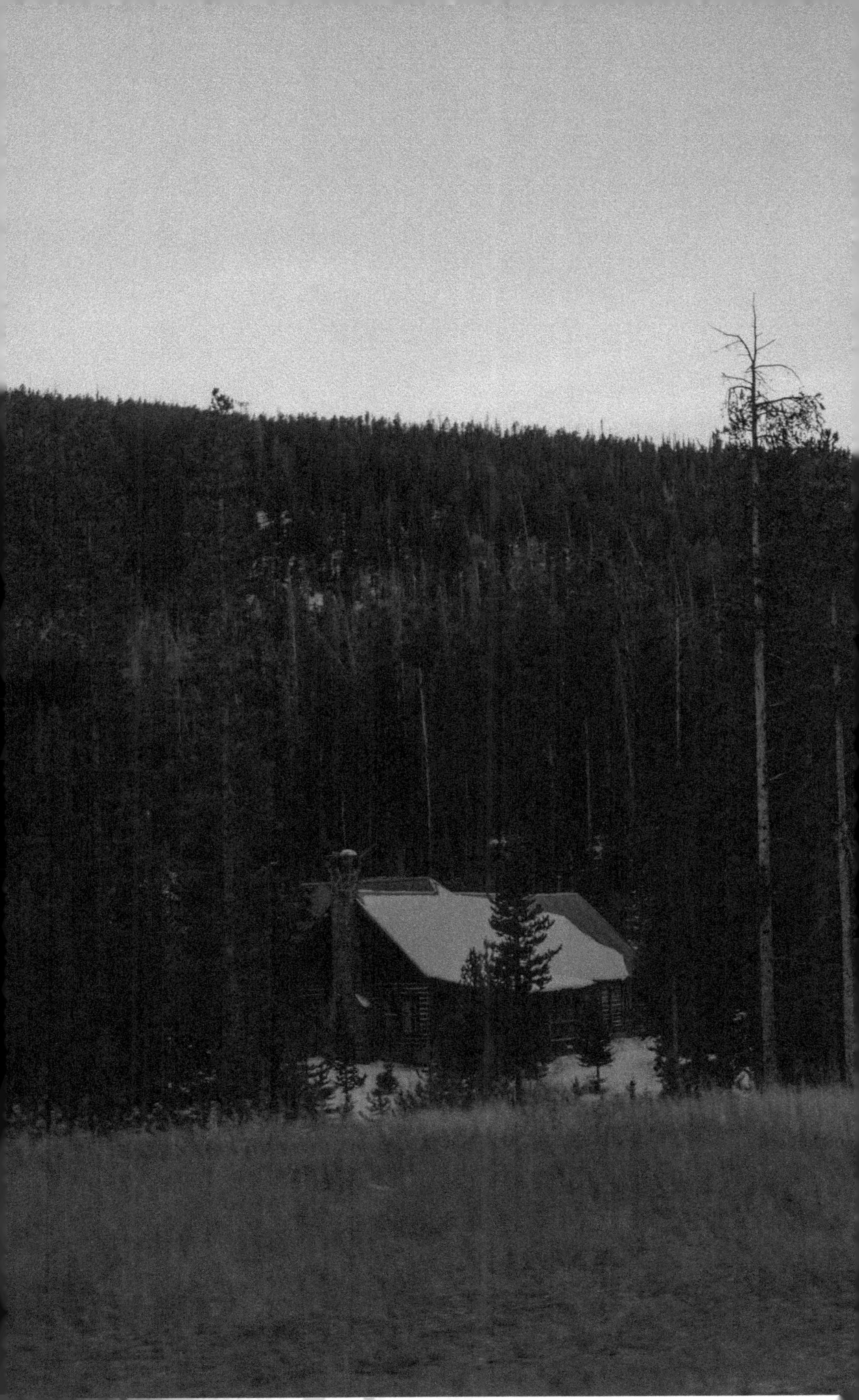

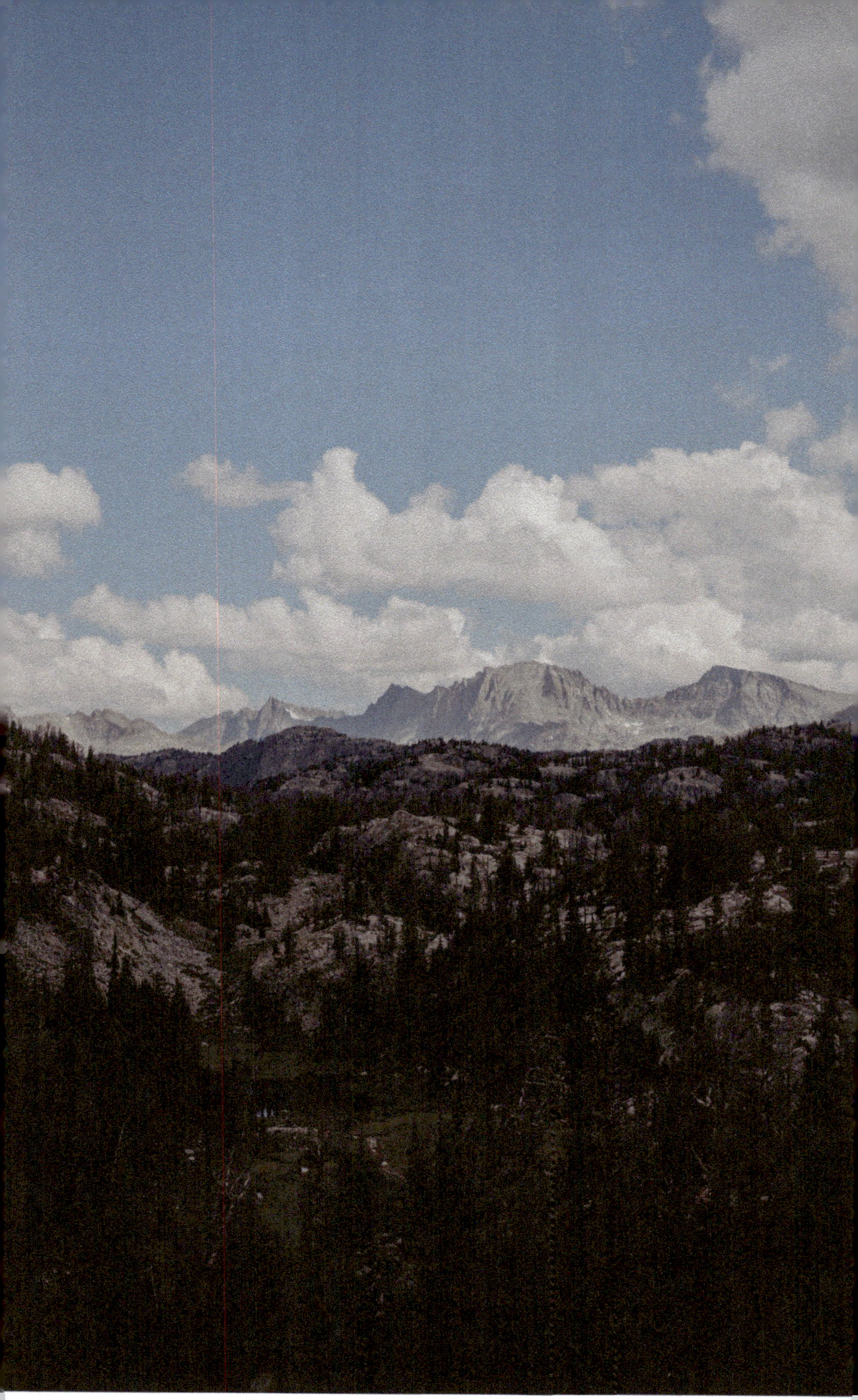

shadows of clouds racing across the land,

make me feel small,

please make me feel small.

the light on the top of the
pine trees,
shadows cast in darkened
valleys,
the mountains unwavering
in their gentle worship,
even the sunlight seems to
whisper,
welcome home.
welcome home.

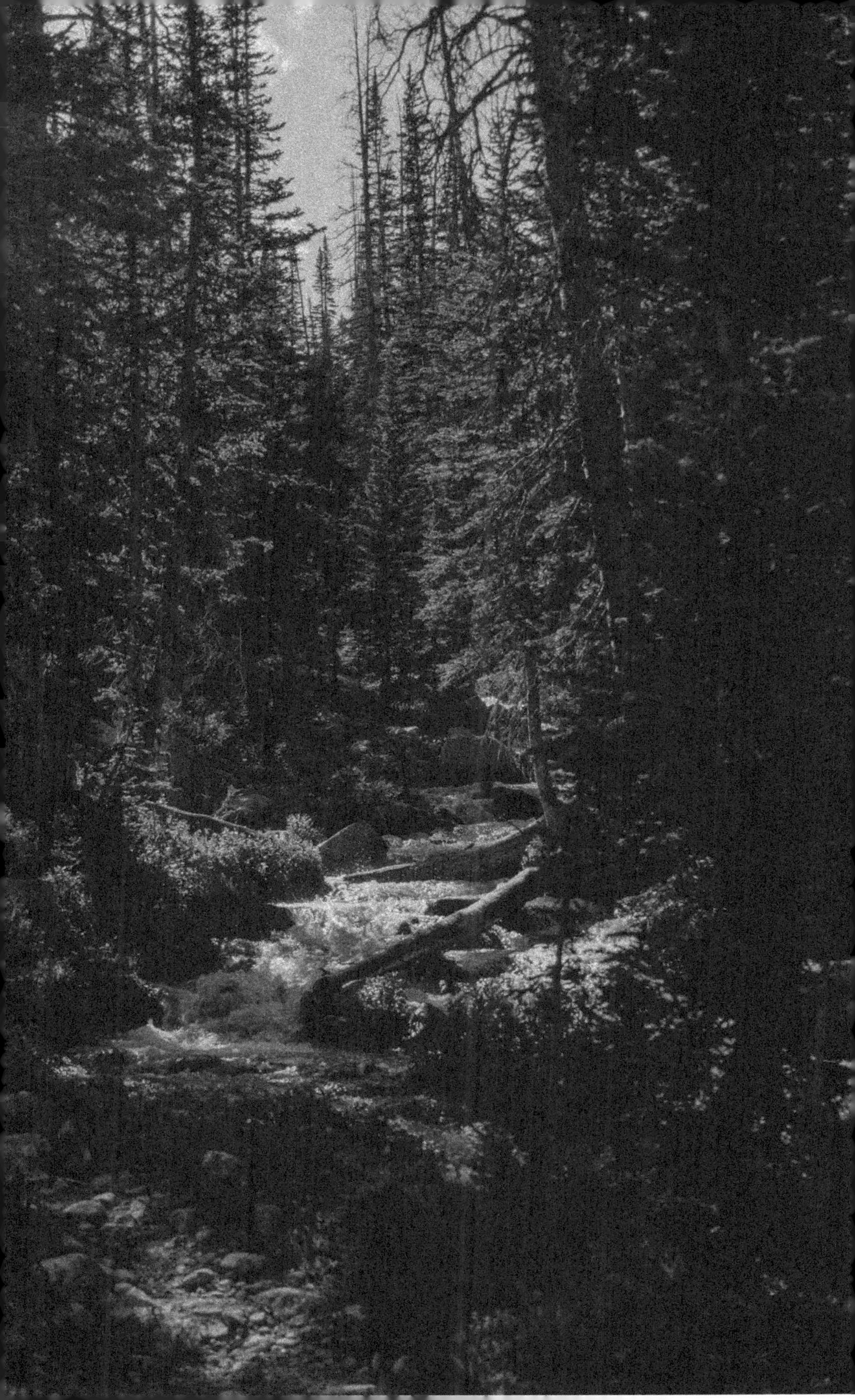

lessons from the plains

the plains are the most insightful of landscapes.
for they are, as the name entails, plain.
they are miles of nothingness, bleak, and dull.

but when in the plains a perplexing emotion exists.
rarely can a place be found where one feels more alone
yet, more at home.

for, when in the mountains, one can find home in the trees, the valleys,
the rocks and caves.
but in the plains, the only place to find a home is in yourself.

when faced with a vast abyss of nothingness you find the only thing to see
is the mutterings of your own mind and the yearnings of your own heart.

among the waving wheat is the wisdom of your own soul.
and the passion of your own innate human desire to exist.

in the plains there is the
pains,
sorrows,
joys,
and exhilarations
of the generations that came before you.
yet, despite the tumultuous existence of their lives, the plains remained.

unchanging, ever present.
unyielding, ever sturdy.
unbreakable, ever growing.
unrelenting in their nothingness but abundant in their own understanding.

for though we stumble, though we live,
we die,
we cry,
we laugh,
we feel at home,
and we feel alone,
the plains just keep swaying, ever so gently, content with being just that,

plain.

people watching

like the sunrise over an open grain field, she lives,
consistent, comfortable, instantly feeling like home.
unaware of her own beauty.
she sees the ocean and wonders why she doesn't wave.
but the sea is far too dangerous, wild and unpredictable.
she is blind to her own perfection.
safety.
simplicity.
joy.
strength.
she may not wave but she also does not waver,
drawing people in,
longing to wander in her depth.

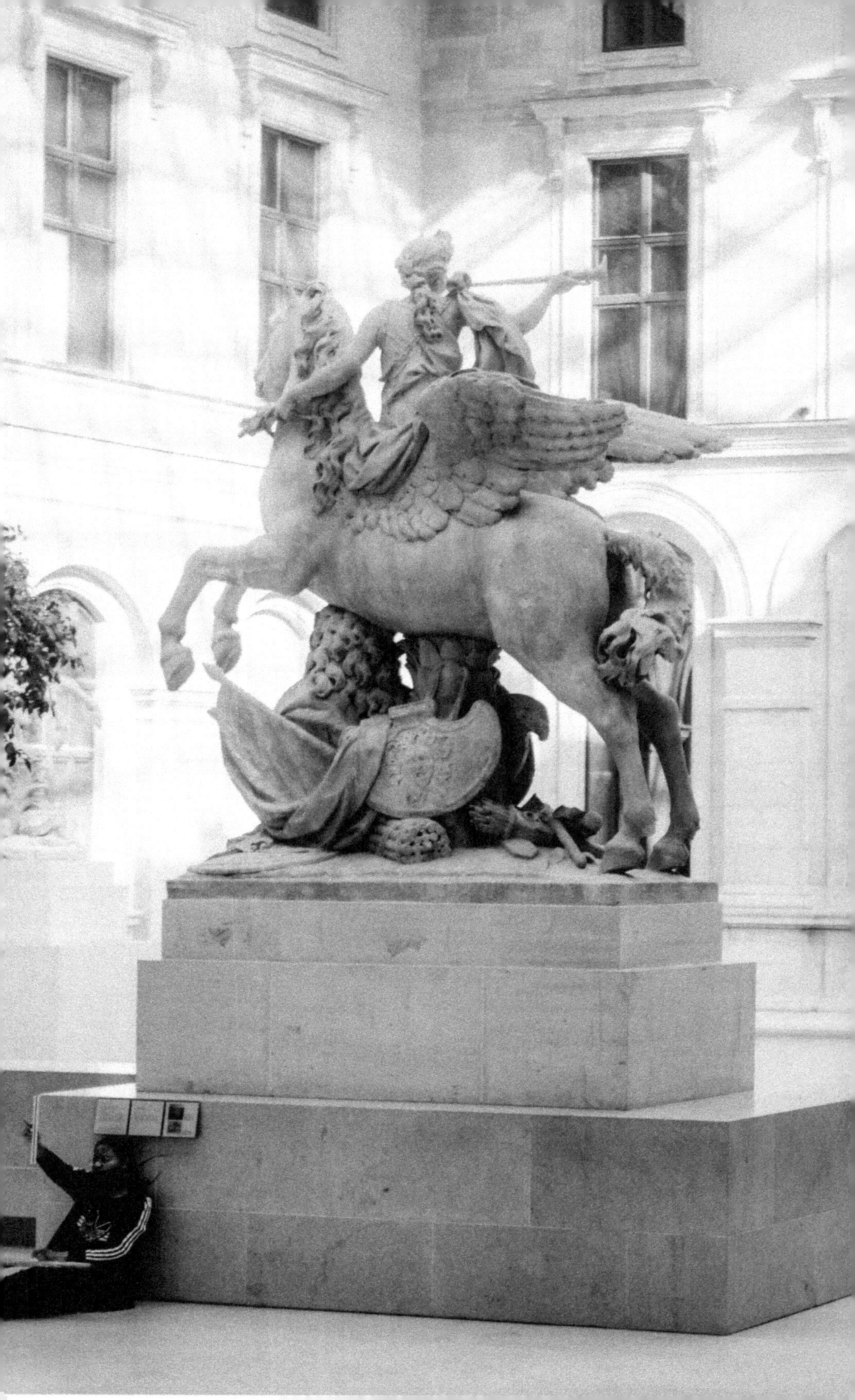

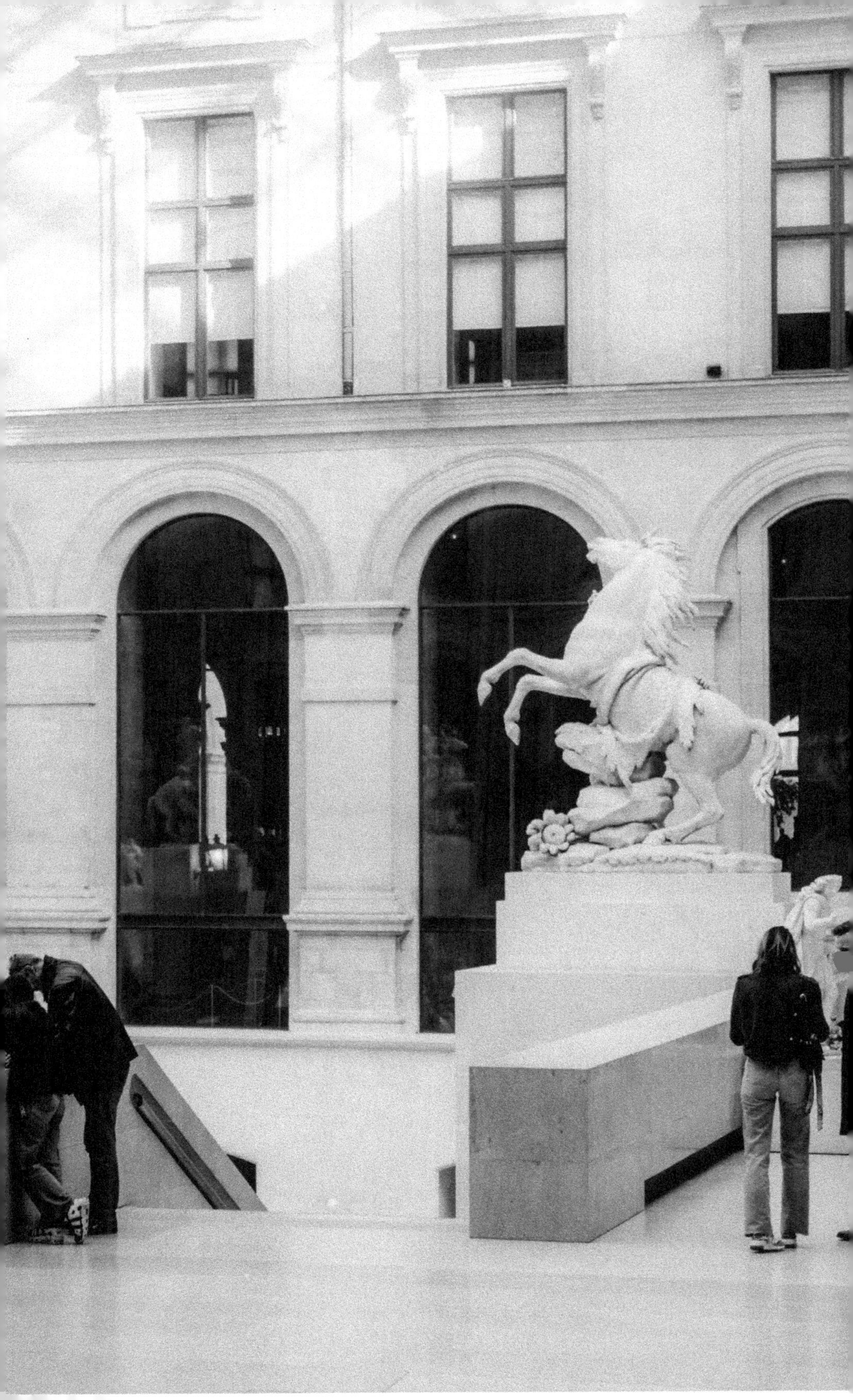

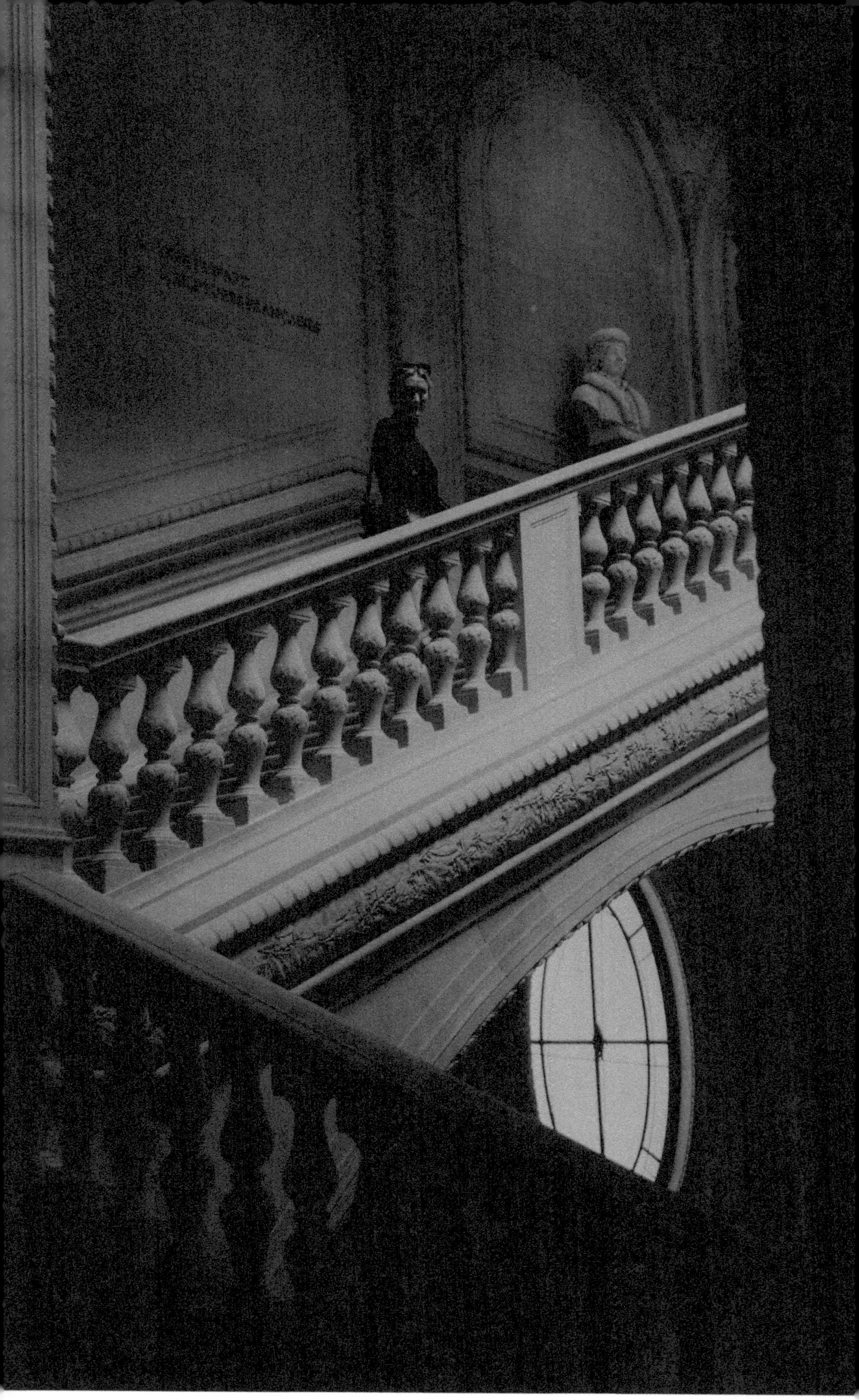

as i wander and write,
rue and reflect,
i discover perhaps simplicity is art,
and contentedness is the meaning of life.

it's going to be ok :)

live in the moments that make you feel alive.
roll your windows down.
sing at the top of your lungs.
get up at sunrise.
drink your coffee black.
stay out too late.
dance like you're alone.
it doesn't matter.
in the end, happiness exists in those tiny
moments of life.

exhaling hallelujah

dance for the moon.
sing for the stars.
recognize His glory wherever you are.
know that while your breaking heart is in reform,
there is change and hope to be found in this storm.
you are loved.
you are whole.
and He who stills the wind, looks after your soul.

unending well

i've spent my whole life looking to belong,
feeling like a misplaced note in the middle of a song.
i mirror others, knowing i am putting on a mask, burdening myself with an impossible task.
adjusting to fit the mold, adapting to the new, abandoning the old.
changing to find a place.
irregular, looking to fit in a regular space.
i've always been a little off, a hard exterior cracked to reveal something broken and soft.
i seek to conform to every situation, changing who i am to match the occasion.
but in ever pouring myself out, i am left empty, parched, in a drought.
feeling like a burden for being who i am,
so i wander like a lost lamb.

but i am one Jesus always sees.
He left the 99 to find me.
with my Heavenly Father my aching heart no longer groans.
and in His arms, i am no longer alone.
i am loved just as i am. He chose me just as much as he chose abraham.
He picked my heart.
He created my soul.
loving not just parts of me but the whole.
in His image i find my worth, allowing my real self to come forth.
sometimes unknown to myself in an effort to please, but known by my father with ease.
i am loved in prosperity, adored as a perfect item of rarity.
i am no longer second best.
i am chosen and selected above the rest.
Jesus left the 99 to find me even though i roam, and in his perfect love,
i find my home.

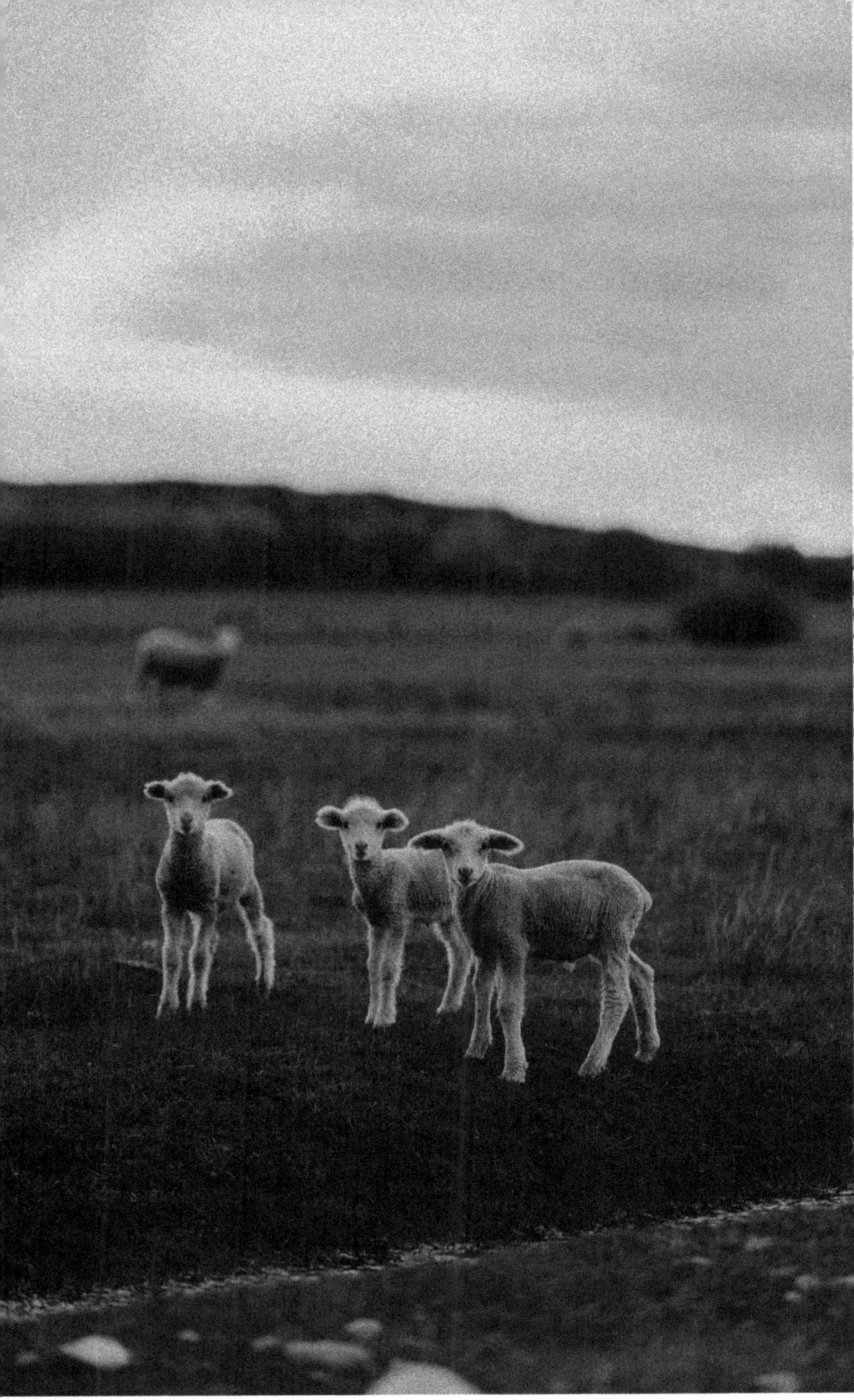

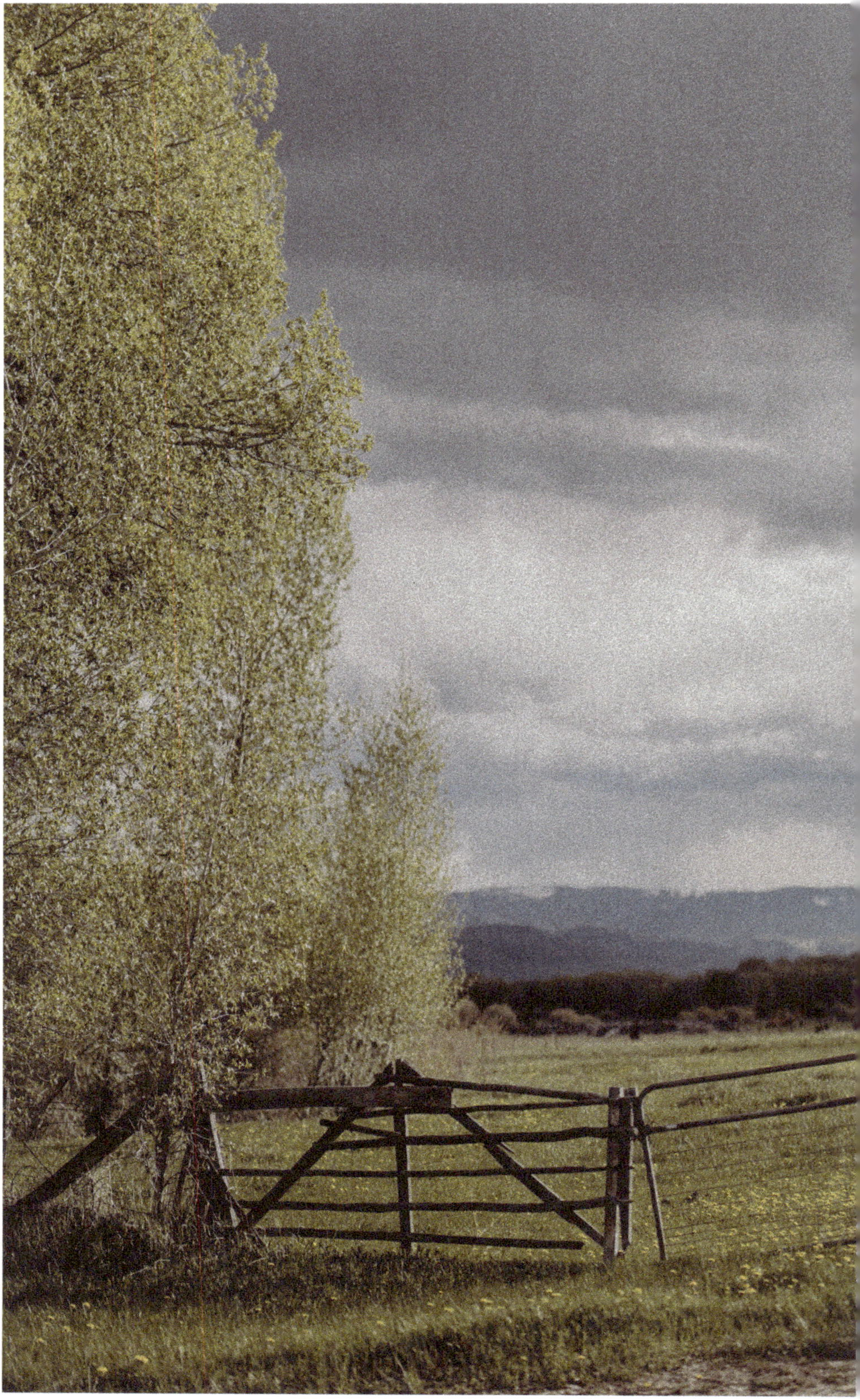

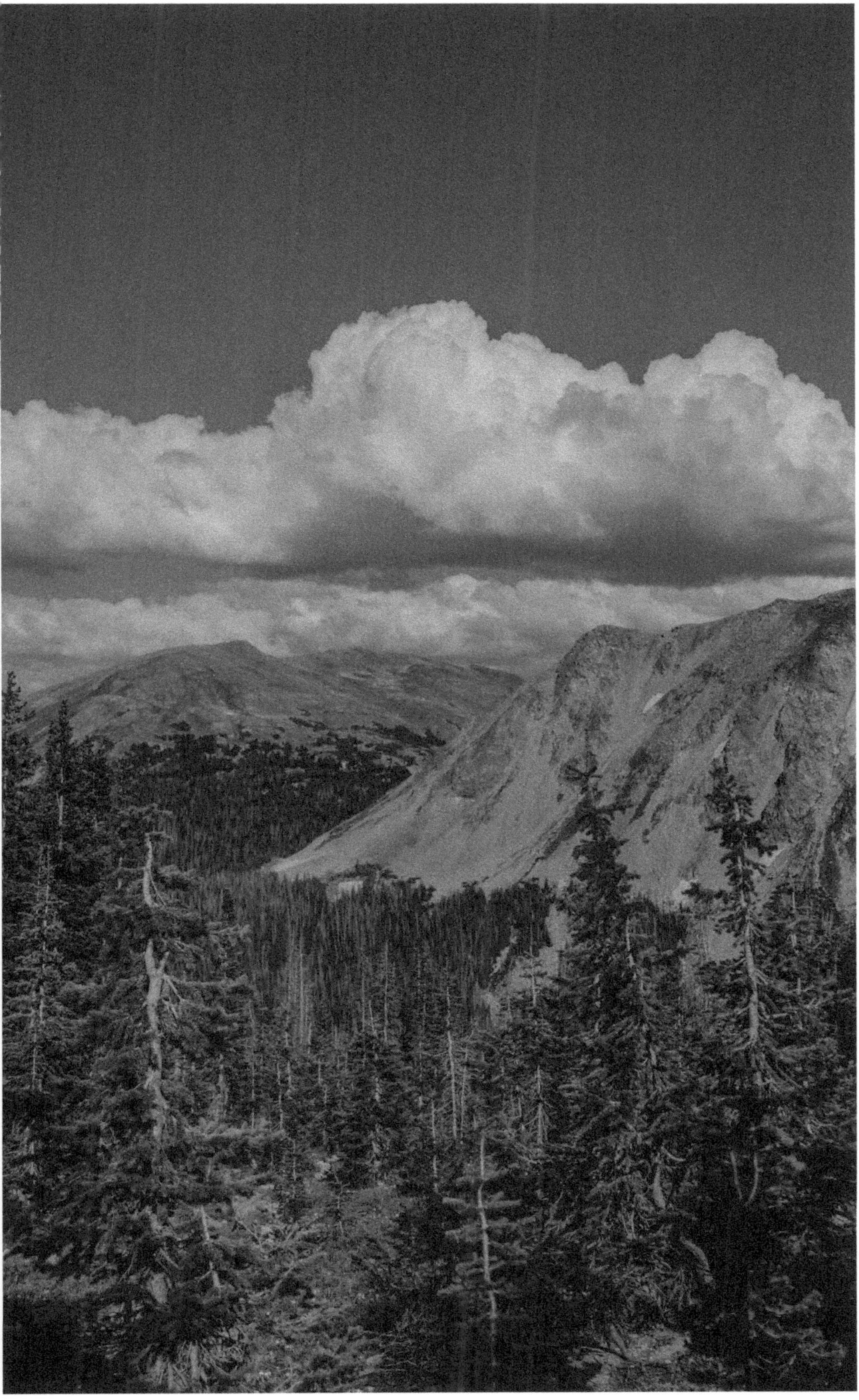

papers in my bible,
tucked between the pages,
in the front cover,
hidden in the seams,
scattered with my mama's handwriting,
feels like home.
feels like home.

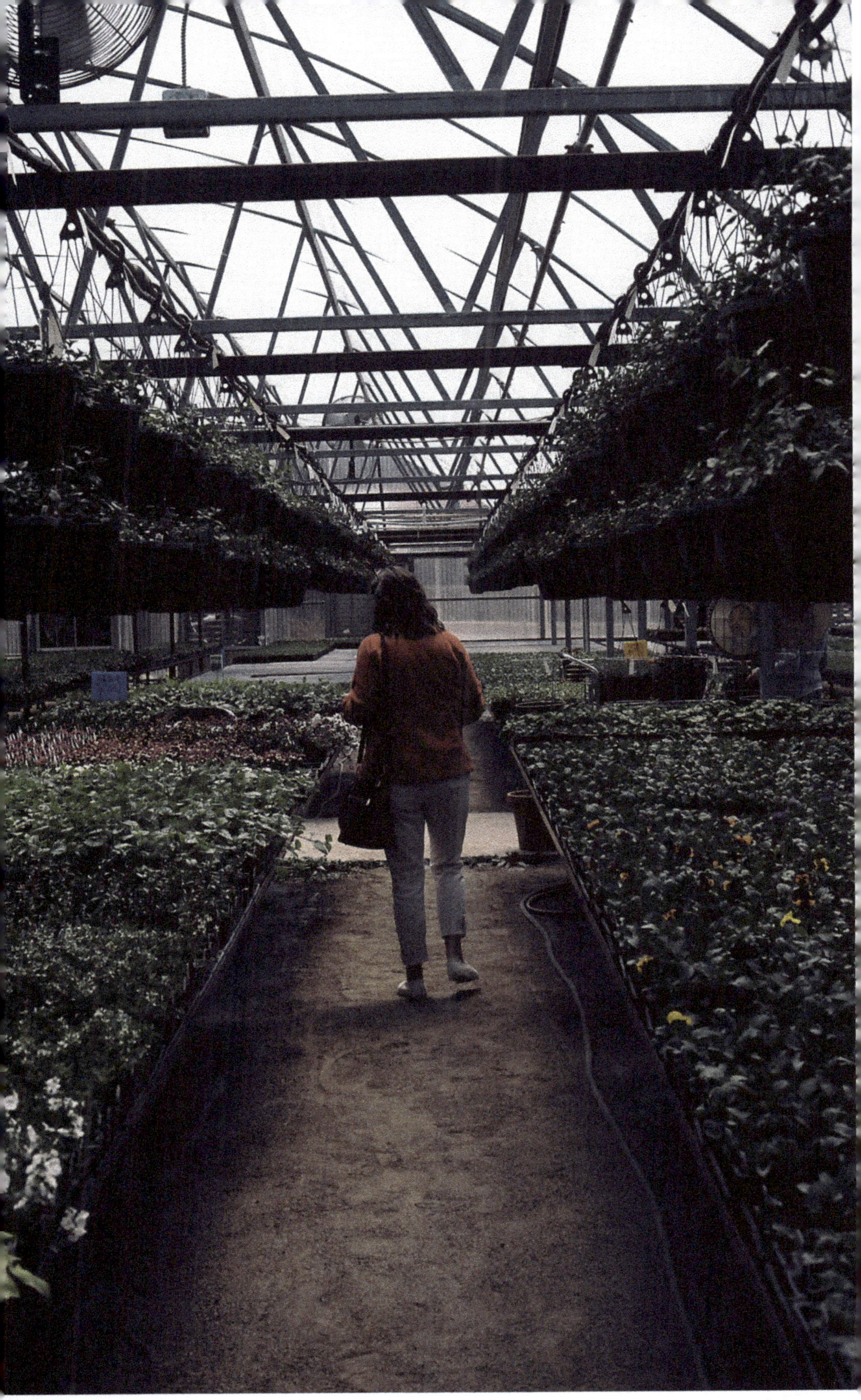

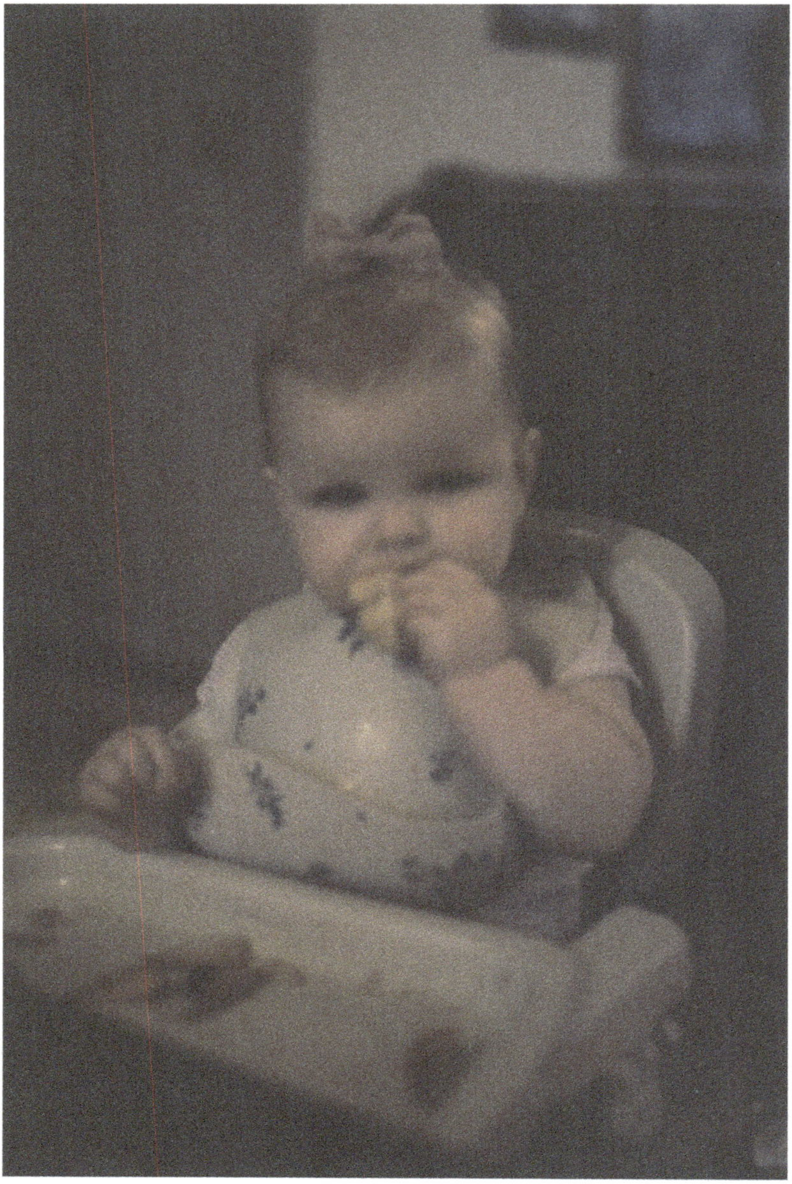

from the mouths of babes

the soft babbles singing along to worship.
dancing to a melody unknown.
unafraid.
unaware.
a child praising the God of all creation.
they don't know to whom they praise.
yet, perhaps they know better than any.
the child-like innocence that is the perfection of faith.
undoubting.
pure.
He said, "let the children come to me."
worshiping.
"they don't know the way of the world."
"they're naive."
oh, how wrong we are.
it is through the eyes of children that we should believe.

the potter

He reached down from the stars,
and dug His fingers deep into the ground
pulling up the purest of clay, soft, malleable, smelling of the earth.
He smiled softly as He began to shape it,
gently using His well-worn hands,
firm, but full of love, dedicated to his craft.
As He worked, He spoke truth into the clay,
"you are made in my image."
"you are fearfully and wonderfully made."
"you are my own."
He worked, tirelessly constructing the clay,
crafting eyes, a nose, hands, and feet.
every single movement purposeful and flawless.
when He finished,
He sat back, pleased with His creation, seeing absolute perfection,
and He breathed life into the clay,
saying, "go and show others my love."
"who are you?" we stammer, unaccustomed to our own voice.
"do not be afraid little one, I am the I am." he replies,
"I am the potter, and you my love, are my clay."

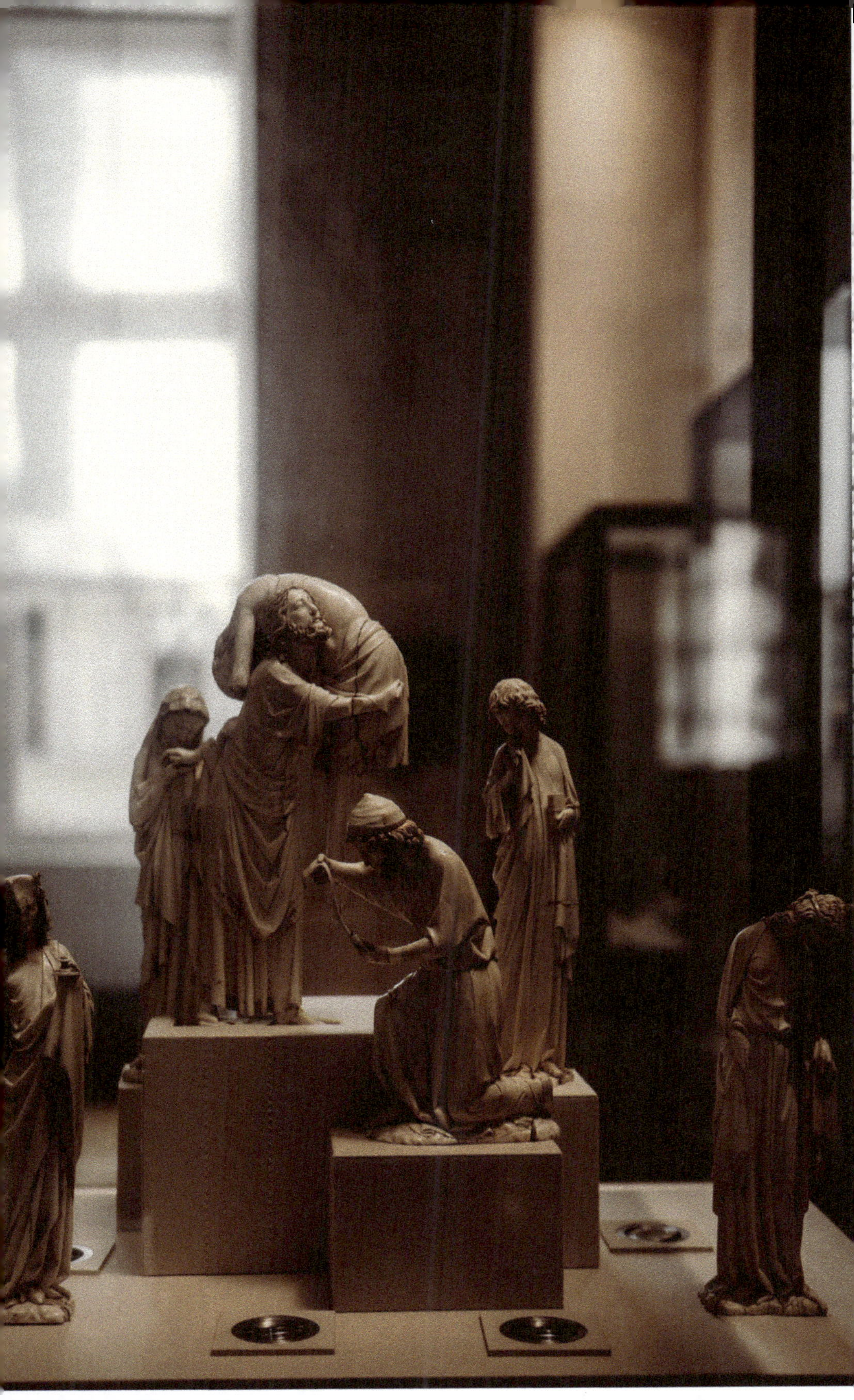

"there is no fear in love. but perfect love drives out fear, because fear has to do with punishment. the one who fears is not made perfect in love."
1 john 4:18

perfect love drives out fear. a statement said so effortlessly yet rich in truths. as a human being, i lack the knowledge of perfect love. i act in fear, wondering when it will all fall apart. knowing deep down the concept of unconditional love exists, perhaps in books and movies but is unobtainable in my own existence. hindered and rendered useless by years of proving myself or working for love, desperate to be loved wholly and honestly, without restraint. yet often times i place too much hope and trust in humanity and find myself disappointed when they finally realize i am not enough and the toiling and desperation i had acted in was all in vain. i live in fear. knowing one day they will see through the facade and find me working endlessly to be seen as worthy in their eyes. i do not rest. i do not find peace. i lie awake dreaming that someday they will see me as i see them, imperfect yet worthy.

but there is a man, who died for me without even knowing me. He sacrificed his life for me in the hope that i would one day desire a relationship with Him. He acted in complete selflessness. loving me limitlessly. without hesitation. in Him my weary heart finds rest. i don't have to fear letting myself be loved. i know i am truly loved by Him, no matter my shortcomings. truly unconditionally. i still find myself pushing that love anyway, finding myself unworthy, deeming myself unloveable. but it's my own insecurities and human error that push Him away. i am scared. i am filled with fear. i do not understand his perfect love. i do not understand why he would choose to pursue and give so much for someone like myself. the voices in my head shout of my failures and berate me with lies. and still, from deep within the recesses of my soul comes a gentle whisper, begging me to rest in His presence, that i am ok with Him. in His eyes, i have no faults. in His eyes i am perfect. He reminds me in the world of His own perfect love. He created the water to reflect the sky so she could be aware of her own beauty. every petal of the flower is crafted with tender artistry. the mountains do not strive to be seen. the thunder feels no hesitation in its voice. the sun is not ashamed of its rays. the trees do not wonder if they are swaying correctly. nature shines in the comfort of perfect love. the serenity of eden was not earned, it was given. the world does not tremble in fear, it rests, flourishes, and grows encased in the ease of unconditional.

i can not comprehend unconditional love. my heart still beats in fear of being shattered, despite being never fully pieced. yet, in my moments of complete despair, when i am drowned by my own voice and can not reach up to grasp desperately for the hand reaching for me, i think of the flowers. they are never punished. they do not labor. they are unafraid. they grow, they exist, they bring joy, and they reach forever skyward praising and hoping to catch a glimpse of the God of perfect love.

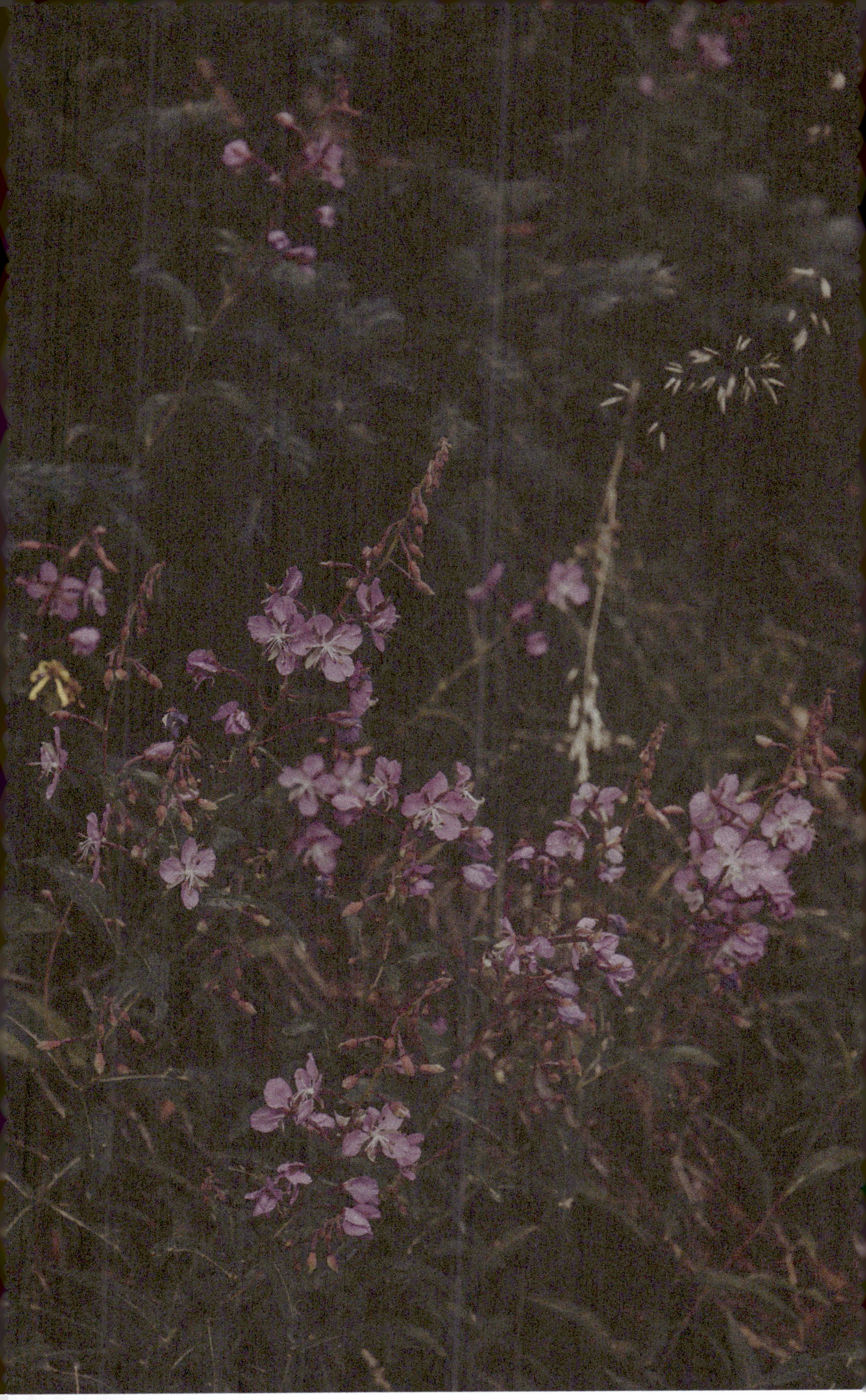

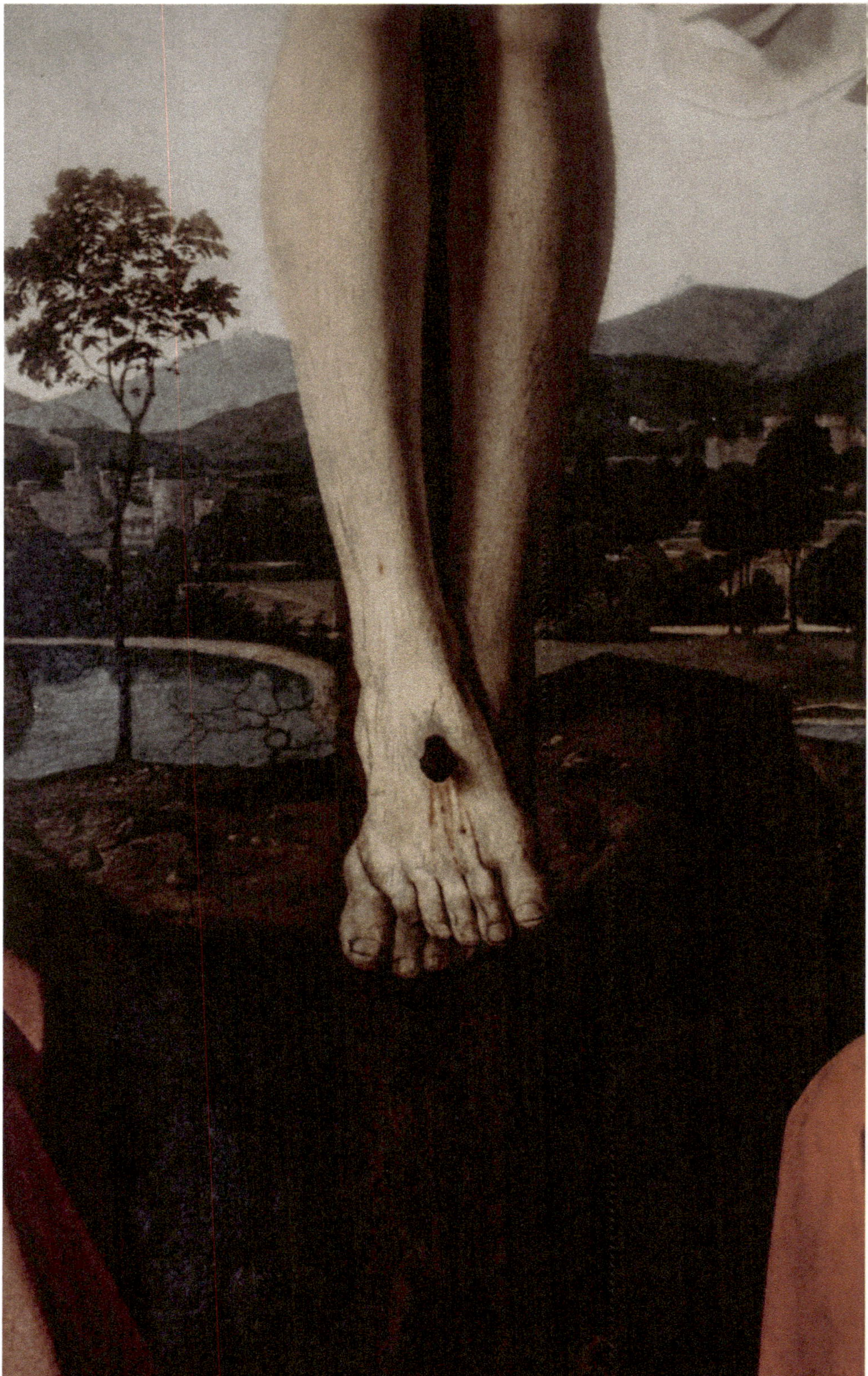

written in red

He speaks to us in red,
and the God of the universe wept, it said.
He who created the birds and the trees,
true love and scraped knees,
He who makes the mountains quake,
He who calls the sun and moon to wake,
wrote to us words of love.
words to give us hope like the branch in the beak of a small white dove,
He blessed us with a timeless book,
so our troubled hearts would know where to look.
yet it is not just a story, it is His heart.
it is the most profound place to start.
it is the words inscribed on your soul
whispering "come to me, I will make you feel whole"

hallelujah.

hallelujah.

hallelujah.

self inflicted stalemate

the battle for self is a struggle between heart and soul.
for the soul is soaked in wisdom, discernment, and truth.
but the heart is feeble,
the heart betrays our hope.
it says we need happiness, worldly desires, and falsities.
but the desires of the heart are fleeting distractions.
the soul longs after contentment, joy, and truth.
the heart craves lust; the soul seeks love.
the heart searches for purpose;
the soul rests in the truth of contentedness.
the heart is momentary; the soul is timeless.
so, my friend, turn away from the desires of your beating heart,
and find rest in the steadiness of your soul.

the stagnant shackles of what if

we find comfort in the questioning.
we ask with empty hearts,
afraid of the answer.
for when we get an answer,
we might have to do the thing we fear most,
change.

we find comfort in the questioning,
because it doesn't challenge us.
it lets us continue to live in the conditioned space of discomfort.
for in the unknown we see safety, ease, and stale familiarity.

we find comfort in the questioning.
for we know once we receive an answer,
our life is no longer our own,
and we must face the simplest yet hardest challenge of all,
truly surrendering,
to the God who already knows our soul.

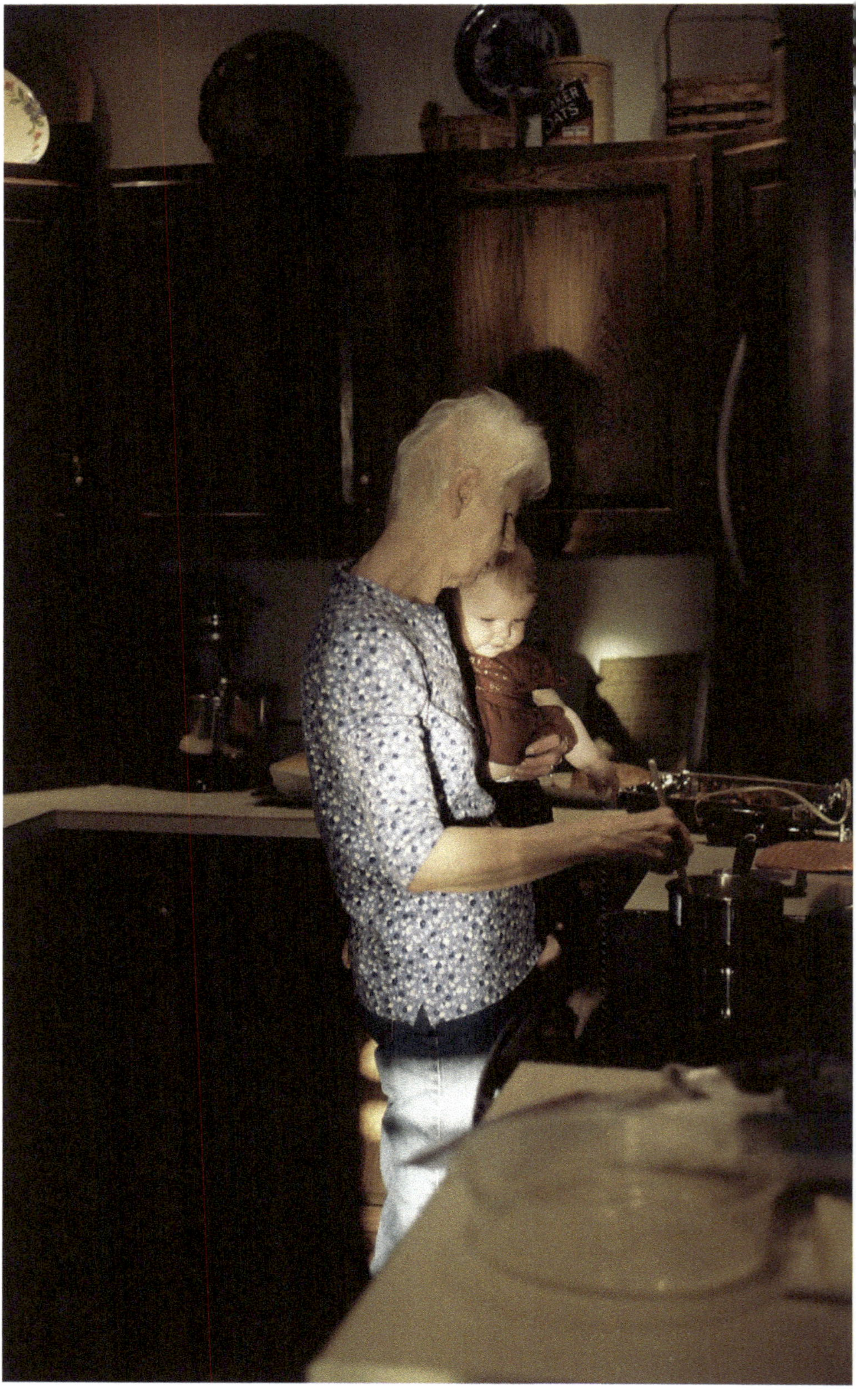

soften

everyone sees their life through their own eyes.
seeing their own reality.
so, when we look upon others,
may we see their perception,
even if different than our own,
before we cast the stones handed to us by our own lives.
for they have lived a life that is their own.
a life we therefore will never understand.
be gentle.
show compassion.
who are we to judge a life we have not lived?

life is beautiful & you do have time

perhaps we are called the human race because we're always running.
towards the next best thing.
towards the hope that something will finally make us happy.
to that success, that fame, that moment of glory.

but,
we run so fast we forget to live.
we focus so much on the finish line we forget to look around.
we forget to see who's running with us.
we forget to appreciate every moment that we even get to be
a part of the race.
we hate our bodies that are carrying us,
despise the ground beneath us,
fear for the next hill.
we forget the perfection that had to take place for us to
simply exist,
we just put our heads down and keep running.

stop.
today, just walk.
look around.
see the sun in the trees.
the beauty of the clouds and the dirt on the ground,
the smiles on strangers' and loved ones' faces,
the pounding of your heart,
the gentle hum of your breath,
the feel of your skin,
the thoughts that exist in the mind that is you,

you are alive.

remember that today.
embrace it in every way.
you only get one, don't waste your human race,
take a deep breath and steady your pace.

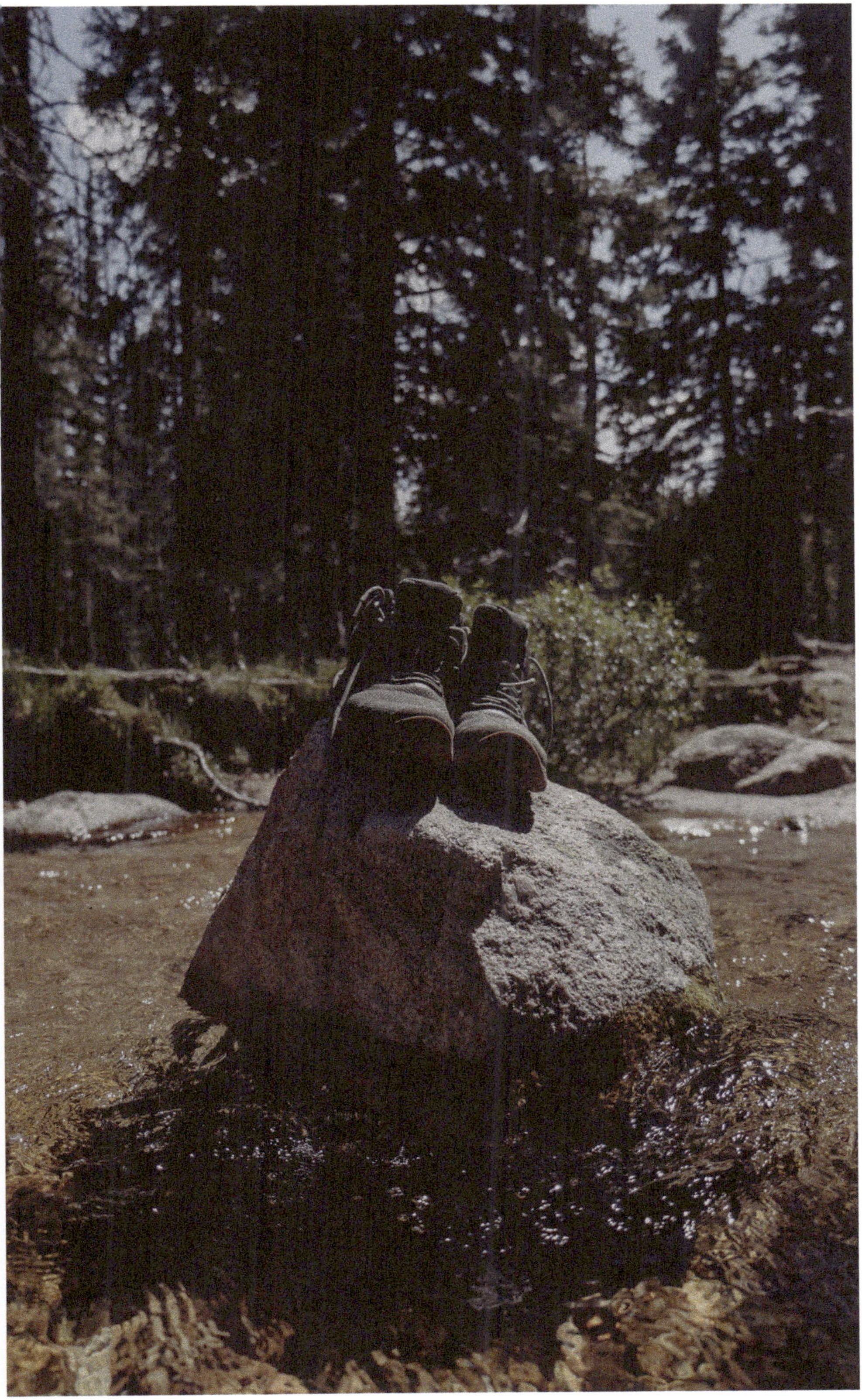

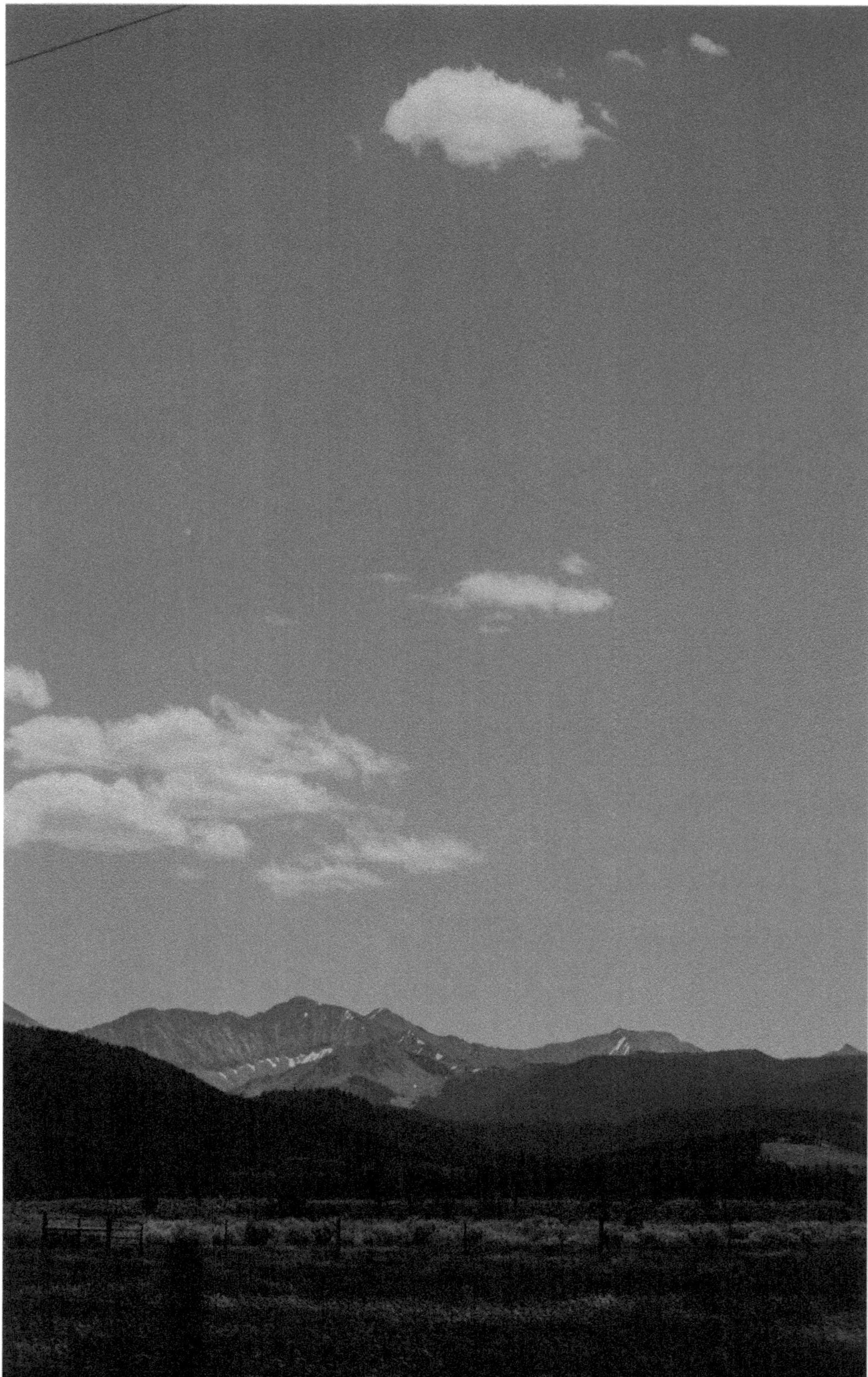

be gentle

if you ever feel sad and don't know why,
i want you to know it's ok to cry,
to have a bad day,
say things you didn't mean to say.
feel the pain in your shoulders,
the emotions dragging you down like boulders.
it takes courage to feel.
lean into the hurt, today you don't have to heal.
just promise me one little thing,
tomorrow, try to hear the birds sing.
on days the world is just too much to bear,
try to bow your head and find hope in prayer.
but, my dear friend, i'm proud of you for simply living today.
so let the tears fall as they may.
it's okay.

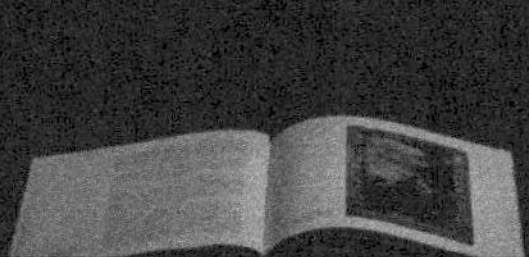

el fin

finishing a book,
is the most bittersweet of actions.
for one feels empty,
and yet so full.
as though something has been ripped away from them.
the melancholy bliss of a story beautifully told.

i wish i was more like orion

i wonder so often if my words have a purpose,
if i am doing the world any service.
then i recognize in the sheer number of words written,
perhaps i can find comfort in being forgotten.
no one can read every story ever told and recorded,
but perhaps my words can mean something to someone,
when they come across them.

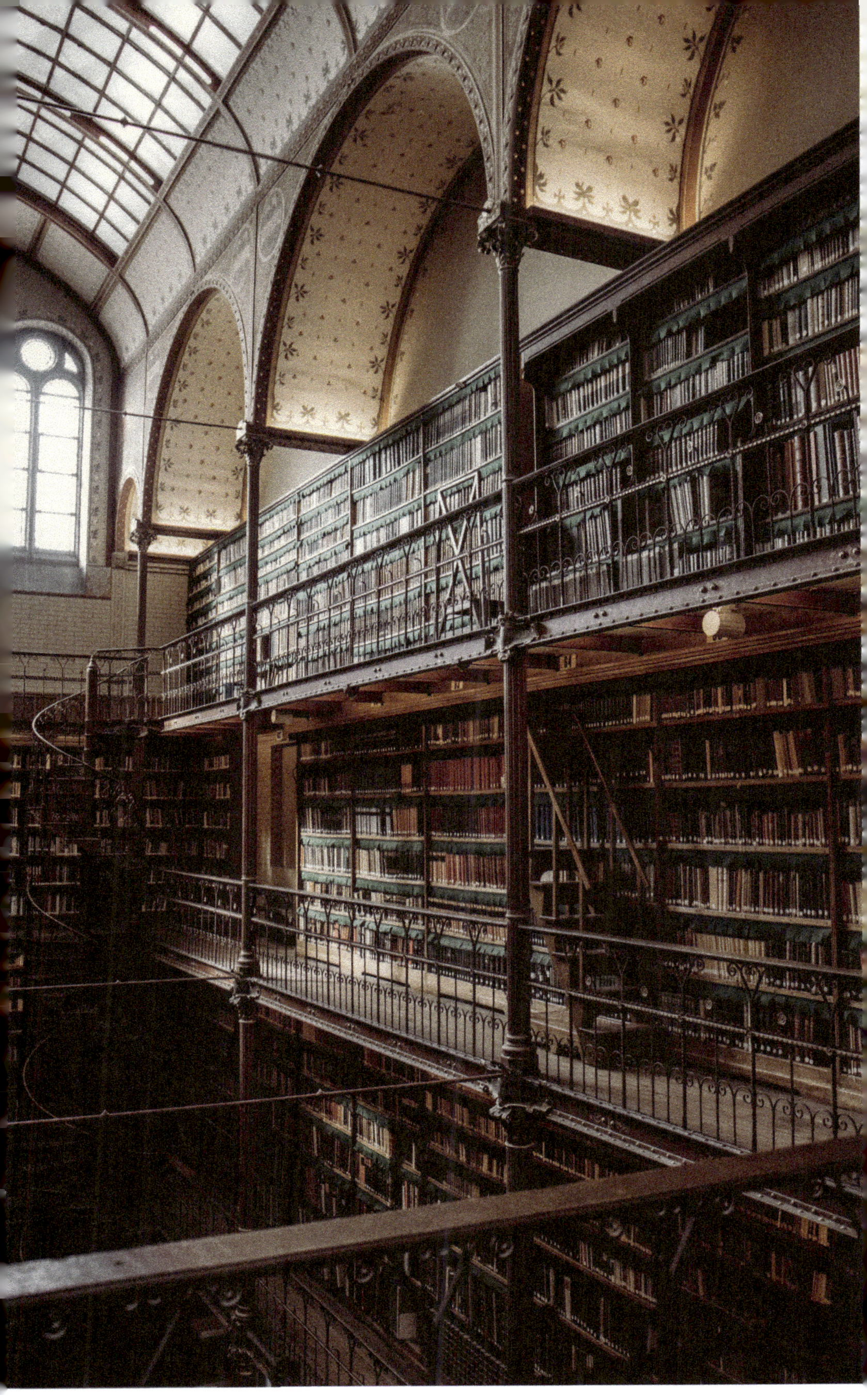

photo catalog

page: adjacent to named poem (if named) : location, country - specific if unique : camera photo was captured on

4: from one soul to another : paris, france - musee rodin : canon 90d
7: wyoming, usa - medicine bow national forest : canon r
8: almost : versailles, france - garden of the palace of versailles : canon 90d
10: paris, france - the louvre : canon 90d
11: paris, france - musee rodin : canon 90d
13: colorado, usa - la plata canyon : canon ae-1 35mm film
14: flicker : paris, france : canon ae-1 35mm film
16: yellowstone national park, usa : canon 90d
17: lubbock, texas : canon 90d
18: crossed constellations: wyoming, usa : canon 90d
21: wyoming, usa : canon r
22 & 23: colorado, usa - la plata canyon : canon ae-1 35mm film
24: the comfort of a slow love : wyoming, usa - wind river range : canon r
26: colorado, usa - my grandmother's house: canon ae-1 35mm film
27: amsterdam, netherlands : canon ae-1 35mm film
29: paris, france - musee rodin : canon 90d
30: maybe home is not a place : versailles, france : canon 90d
33: liquid soul : paris, france - musee rodin : canon 90d
36 & 37: wyoming, usa : canon r
42: my first friday night without you : colorado, usa : canon ae-1 35mm film
44: wyoming, usa : canon r
45: wyoming, usa : canon r
47: versailles, france : canon 90d
49: colorado, usa : canon 90d
51: maybe i said too much...maybe i didn't say enough : wyoming, usa : canon r
52: wyoming, usa - medicine bow national forest : canon r

55: icarus : paris, france : canon 90d
57: to the death of a dream : paris, france - the louvre : canon ae-1 35mm film
59: glass bubble bath : wyoming, usa : canon r
60: utah, usa - canyonlands national park : canon r
65: predator : versailles, france - garden of the palace of versailles : canon 90d
66: paris, france - musee rodin : canon 90d
69: versailles, france - garden of the palace of versailles : canon 90d
73: versailles, france - garden of the palace of versailles : canon 90d
74: a dream of my inner child : unknown : unknown
77: clutches : wyoming, usa - medicine bow national forest : canon r
85: careful casting : paris, france - musee rodin : canon ae-1 35mm film
86: colorado, usa - aj's greenhouse : canon ae-1 35mm film
87: colorado, usa : canon 90d
90: colorado, usa - aj's greenhouse : canon ae-1 35mm film
91: colorado, usa - aj's greenhouse : canon ae-1 35mm film
93: versailles, france - garden of the palace of versailles : canon 90d
99: and so to is the cycle of leaves : wyoming, usa : canon r
101: run away and don't come back : wyoming, usa - medicine bow national forest : canon r
102: colorado, usa : canon ae-1 35mm film
104 & 105: versailles, france: canon 90d
106 & 107: wyoming, usa - grand teton national park: canon 90d
109: reverie : wyoming, usa - medicine bow national forest: canon r
110: wyoming, usa: canon r
113: colorado, usa: canon r
116 & 117: paris, france - the louvre : canon 90d
118: paris, france - the louvre : canon 90d
123: unending well : wyoming, usa : canon r
124: wyoming, usa : canon r
125: colorado, usa : canon r
127: colorado, usa - aj's greenhouse : canon ae-1 35mm film
128: from the mouth of babes : colorado, usa : canon ae-1 35mm film
131: the potter : paris, france - the louvre : canon 90d
133: wyoming, usa : canon r
134: written in red : paris, france - the louvre : canon 90d
139: soften : colorado, usa : canon ae-1 35mm film
140: life is beautiful & you do have time : colorado, usa : canon r
142: be gentle : colorado, usa : canon r
144: el fin : paris, france - the louvre : canon 90d
147: i wish i was more like orion : amsterdam, netherlands : canon 90d

CPSIA information can be obtained
at www.ICGtesting.com
Printed in the USA
LVHW081726210423
745008LV00006B/750

9 781957 864808